Has Anybody Here Seen Kelly?

In Search of My Father

Joe Cushnan

Published in 2021
by FeedARead.com Publishing

This research and writing project has been supported by funds from the National Lottery through the Arts Council of Northern Ireland

LOTTERY FUNDED

For future Cushnans and their connections, so they can understand a little of their family's past.

Has anybody here seen Kelly?
K E double-L Y.
Has anybody here seen Kelly?
Find him if you can!
C. W. Murphy and Will Letters (1908)

CONTENTS

PROLOGUE

The film *I Never Sang For My Father* (1970), starring
Gene Hackman and Melvyn Douglas, is a powerful human
story, beautifully scripted and performed. The plot revolves
around a complicated and emotional father/son
relationship. The nub of the story concerns a decision by
the son to move to America's West Coast, leaving his
widowed father alone in New York. One line has stuck
with me over the years. Gene Hackman, the son, struggling
with his father's predicament and fear of loneliness, says: 'I
hate him. And I hate to hate him.'

While I have been researching and writing this memoir, I
have often thought of those words with regards to my own
father. As I uncover more about his life, I wonder what my
conclusions will be in the final chapter. Will I choose to use
the word 'hate'? The plot of the film is not quite the same
as my story, but it's interesting nonetheless. One other
thing the Gene Hackman character says after his father's
death made me think: 'Death ends a life, but it does not end
a relationship, which struggles on in the survivor's mind
towards some resolution, which it may never find.' How
powerful is that?

I was also struck by the chemistry in John Mortimer's
play *A Voyage Round My Father*. The father in this play
loses his sight in an accident, and as result of which he is
dependent on those around him to assist whenever he needs
help. The father, a barrister, is opinionated and irritable, but
he also carries around a lot of wisdom which he imparts
liberally. The relationships within the family are stiff, cold
and unemotional. His son becomes a barrister too and
increasingly resembles his father in word and action, even
though their relationship has never been particularly deep

or serious. The final act sees the father take his last breath while the son reflects on the father who is no longer there:

> I'd been told of all the things you
> are meant to feel. Sudden freedom,
> growing up, the end of dependence,
> the step into sunlight when no one
> is taller than you and you're in no
> one's shadow. I know what I felt.
> Lonely.[1]

It is a very powerful play, and a reminder that family relationships often have more faces than Big Ben and the Albert Clock combined.

The poet Seamus Heaney had very fond memories of his father, as reflected in some of his poetry. In the poem 'Follower', the young boy observes his father plough a field:

> All I ever did was follow
> In his broad shadow around the
> farm.
>
> I was a nuisance, tripping, falling,
> Yapping always. But today
> It is my father who keeps stumbling
> Behind me, and will not go away.[2]

---

[1] John Mortimer, *A Voyage Round My Father* (first published 1971).
[2] Extract from 'Follower', first published in Seamus Heaney, *Death of a Naturalist* (1966).

The point is, he admired his father and he had a role model to grow up with and reflect upon for the rest of his life. 'Mid-Term Break' recalls the death of Heaney's four-year-old brother. When young Seamus arrives home from school, he sees another side to his father:

> In the porch I met my father crying.
> He had always taken funerals in his
> stride.[3]

It was okay for a tough farmer to be human and show emotion. As I re-read *Death of a Naturalist*, the 'father' poems made me feel a little envious of this father and this son.

In setting the scene for this memoir I was also drawn to the painting *And When Did You Last See Your Father?* by William Frederick Yeames. The painting allegedly depicts a Royalist family captured by the enemy. The boy in blue is 'in the dock', being questioned about the whereabouts of his father, considered a traitor by the Parliamentarians. If I was the young boy in blue and I had been asked that question when I was six, I wouldn't have had a clue about the answer, as you will soon see.

Sigmund Freud coined the term 'infantile amnesia' to describe his theory that, until the age of six, children either forget or hide their earliest memories. They are either blocked or withheld, but not completely erased. Freud described this as repression. As children approach their teenage years, they remember more than they realise, but as

---

[3] Extract from 'Mid-Term Break', first published in Seamus Heaney, *Death of a Naturalist* (1966).

they grow into adulthood and the decades pass, the early memories really do fade away.

Why am I mentioning this here? Well, when I was six my father left us; as I write I am heading into my mid-sixties. I have racked my brain and tried to recall as many details from my childhood as I can. I'm convinced that I do remember some things. Occasionally a forgotten memory has been triggered by someone else's recollections; sometimes, though, I'm aware that I may well have hijacked someone else's memories and claimed them as my own. It's difficult, too, to disentangle family stories, repeated over and over and over again, from fact. The problem is, there is very little 'fact' to go on.

In this memoir I have the urge to do a couple of things. I am interested in detective mystery stories and, leaving my personal connection to the 'missing person' aside, this is a pretty good mystery to investigate. Why did this man disappear? Where did he go? What did he do? Who were his new friends? Did he have a second family? Did he have a relationship or relationships with other women? Did he have other children? But I also feel a responsibility to research and record this aspect of the Cushnan family history to share my findings with Cushnans down the line. Will this bring any kind of closure? I don't know, but I have found out a considerable amount about my father, my mother and their forebears, information I would never have known had I not embarked on this project.

This memoir, then, is a mixture of conscious recall, fact, and a lively imagination. It is both true and accurate, and a fabrication, much like the man it seeks to find.

CHAPTER 1: Grave Thoughts

On Monday 19 July 1982 it was mild and cloudy at Lambeth Cemetery, London.

I was living in Hemel Hempstead at the time and my brother Kevin was over from Belfast for a business meeting. We met up and travelled together to Clapham as representatives of the Cushnan family for the funeral of our father, John. He died at the age of 57 from an intracranial tumour. At the funeral, all the people there knew him better than Kevin and I did. Jim Nicholson, landlord at the Rose and Crown, our father's local, had informed my mother of her husband's death. She wanted nothing to do with the funeral, with very good reason.

At some point in 1960, my father left his wife and seven young children in Belfast and pretty much vanished. The next we heard of him was when we were told of his death, twenty-two years later.

I was six when he left and Kevin was two. This dead man in Clapham was, to all intents and purposes, a stranger to us both.

We spent the day of the funeral surrounded by his friends, there because they knew and liked our father. But for us, there was only a bizarre emptiness. We were playing the role of mourners. I am reminded of T. S. Eliot, from Four Quartets:

> Home is where one starts from. As
> we grow older
> The world becomes stranger, the
> pattern more complicated

Of dead and living.[4]

I have never felt comfortable in graveyards. The nearest one to home when I was growing up in Andersonstown, Belfast, was Milltown Cemetery. It is where most of my deceased relatives, including my mother, my eldest brother and my grandparents, are buried. A predominantly Catholic graveyard, Milltown is situated between the top end of the Falls Road and the M1 motorway and covers nearly sixty acres. It dates back to the mid-1800s and houses (if that's the correct term) the remains of over two hundred thousand people in around fifty thousand graves. Despite being a 'resting place', Milltown has had its troubling incidents in the past, the best known being when Michael Stone, a member of the Ulster Defence Association (UDA), attacked mourners at the funeral of three IRA members on 16 March 1988. He shot around the crowd randomly and threw hand grenades. Three people were killed and over sixty were wounded. Stone was arrested and eventually jailed. Northern Ireland's 'Troubles' were pretty horrific over the years, but there are still some incidents that send shivers down the spine. I still associate Milltown with the chill of howling winds, miserable drizzle and, on the ghosts' angrier days, pelting rain.

There is obvious sadness in graveyards, especially when remembering one's own kin and friends. They would not be my first choice of location for a day out. But in my more mature years, a walk alone through the tombstones in any cemetery is both meditative and calming.

---

[4] From *Four Quartets* (1943).

Entrance to Lambeth Cemetery, London

On Saturday 3 December 2016, I was walking through Lambeth Cemetery, near St. George's Hospital, London, talking into a small voice recorder. There was no one else above ground, so I wasn't disturbing anyone or attracting the attention of any curious onlookers; those below ground were past caring. It was a lovely cold morning, and the weather was settled and pleasant, a first for me in a graveyard.

The cemetery is a higgledy-piggledy assembly of well-maintained graves, elaborate headstones, floral arrangements, sweet, loving inscriptions, intermingled with neglected plots, their headstones leaning in precarious positions, beds of weeds, engravings worn away by time. There are around 250,000 graves, quite a few, I'm told, occupied by Victorian music hall performers such as comedian, actor and one-time clog dancer Dan Leno, and Stanley Lupino, actor, dancer and writer, and father of

Hollywood star Ida. I tried to think of a cheap music hall connection to describe my father's vanishing act. I came up with the 1908 song 'Has Anybody Here Seen Kelly?'

David Walden, from Lambeth Cemetery office, had looked into my enquiry about my father's grave location. The plot number is 319 in section C2, recorded in the register as burial number 21341. David had alerted me to the fact that there is no headstone.

My father's unmarked grave, Lambeth Cemetery, London

So, there I was, walking around trying to pinpoint his last resting place – his last known address. I finally decided that a patch of bare ground was the spot. I stood there for several minutes and remembered that the last time I had been there was on that Monday in July 1982, with Kevin and a reasonable crowd of mourners, at my father's funeral. I recalled not feeling much sadness at the graveside back then, and on this December morning, thirty-four years later, I didn't feel any different. There were no tears from his sons in 1982 and none from me in 2016 – sad but true. I even tried to force myself to cry. I stood staring at the ground wishing at least one tear would fall. I pictured his face from the few old photographs we have of him; I ran his story through my head, and thought about his selfishness and the distress he caused my mother. I considered the callousness and ruthlessness of his decision to abscond. He was uncaring, heartless, cruel and insensitive. I felt no sorrow at all for this man; there was certainly no sense of loss but possibly a level of contempt. No matter how much I tried, my eyes stayed dry and my emotions remained in check. 'Come not, when I am dead / To drop thy foolish tears upon my grave, / To trample round my fallen head, / And vex the unhappy dust thou wouldst not save', wrote Tennyson in 1842.

'I'm probably only a few feet away from his bones,' I told the voice recorder. 'Somewhere down there, somewhere down there.' It was the closest I had been to him in fifty-six years.

In 1982, there wasn't an opportunity to see the body before the coffin lid was screwed down, the usual farewell tradition back home. Perhaps if I had seen his body, I might have had different feelings towards him. Maybe witnessing his stone-cold corpse would have stirred me. Maybe the tears would have come easily.

It's not that I'm an unemotional man. I have cried at the deaths of family members, friends – even at the passing of Elvis Presley. I can get very emotional listening to music, reading sad stories and watching films. I'm not sure what it says about me that I can't stir up any sign of sadness at the thought of my dead father – I will leave that to the psychologists. I have thought more than once, when re-reading drafts of this manuscript, that he did not deserve my tears. He certainly did not earn them.

As I looked at the bare gravesite, it occurred to me that even with all his new-found friends in London in the 1970s, no one cared enough about him to put some kind of a marker on his grave. I wondered, too, if any of those friends ever came back to the grave over the years to spend a few minutes with their pal. The cemetery's maintenance team runs a lawn mower over the patch of ground in their upkeep routines, so my father's grave is tidy enough. I wonder if they are aware that there is a body down there. For a long time, this seemingly empty patch of ground has probably been a shortcut from one marked grave to another. I considered buying a bunch of flowers to lay on the site but I decided that would be both cynical and hypocritical.

If he had a headstone, what would it say? 'Here lies the body of John Cushnan', or 'Here lies the body of John Kelly.' And the epitaph? It would be too easy to drift into sarcasm with a pithy one-liner, so I'll let that one hang.

I said a few more things into the voice recorder – describing the surroundings and conditions. I thought I was whispering but I must have been speaking at a reasonable volume for a woman about thirty yards away called over: 'Ah, recording memories. So important. God bless.' She was resting on one knee by a rather colourful, neat grave. It had a solid, shiny, black headstone with gold inscriptions. It was quite grand among the various markers in section C2. She was holding a small watering can. I waved the recorder in the air and smiled. I'm not sure if I had ever smiled in a cemetery before. I hoped she wasn't going to be a chatty type because I wanted this time on my own to contemplate. Thankfully, she waved back without a word and got on with the task of making the tidy grave even tidier. What a contrast, I thought as I looked back at my father's rather miserable anonymous grassy patch.

So, I knew that my father started life in the New Lodge area of Belfast in 1925 and I knew that he ended up in plot 319, Lambeth Cemetery, in 1982. That was something.

This research and writing task has been a little like constructing a jigsaw puzzle, getting all the straight-edged pieces into a frame and then working on the details. It has proven to be, after Lieutenant Columbo, a series of just-one-more-thing clues leading to more clues leading to people and memories and stories – and a few facts.

I spent about half an hour at the gravesite that day, walking around it, staring at it, talking into the recorder and jotting a few things into a notebook. I came across a note I'd made a few weeks earlier. It was a quotation from Colum McCann's book *TransAtlantic*: 'We return to the lives of those who've gone before us, until we come home eventually to ourselves.'[5]

I walked towards the cemetery gates and never looked back.

[5] Colum McCann, *TransAtlantic* (London: Bloomsbury, 2013).

CHAPTER 2: A Blue Folder

The Rose & Crown, Clapham, London

In 2013, I sat in my study staring at an array of items laid out on the desk. Stored in a ragged blue folder, the items had been buried in a filing cabinet drawer since 1982 when the folder was presented to Kevin and me at our father's wake in the Rose & Crown. The folder contained:

- undertaker's receipts;
- an employer's letter;
- a wage slip;
- eight floral bouquet cards;
- one mass card;

- five club membership cards and five payment receipts;
- a note on a scrap of paper;
- two letters from friends;
- correspondence from the Department of Health and Social Security;
- a cheque book and a paying-in bank book;
- nine photographs;
- an empty wallet.

These are the only things my father left behind. It is a rather pathetic inventory; nevertheless, most of the items turned out to be useful in researching his life.

Back at the wake, Kevin and I were in the company of strangers who were shaking our hands with gusto and passing on warm thoughts and happy memories as they reminisced about their recently departed friend. He sounded like a great guy – witty, generous when he could afford to be, and everybody's pal. He had been living, working and mixing with Irish folks far from home in the Big Smoke and was being lauded and mourned by his circle in a boozer not far from Clapham Common. In true Irish fashion, this was a fond farewell, a celebration of a life, maudlin to a point but peppered with stories and a few homesick songs to send his spirit on its way. It was fuelled by free-flowing beer with wee chasers of whiskey and rum, trays of ham and tomato sandwiches and lots of watery-eyed throwaway plaudits: 'Ach, sure, he was a great fella, right enough'; 'One in a million, one in a million.'

Mourning is hard work when you don't know the person you're supposed to be mourning.

Someone handed us the blue folder containing the rather sorry collection of bits and pieces.

'Kelly would have wanted you to have this,' they said.

Kevin and I looked at each other. Kelly? Who the hell was Kelly? We thought we were at the wrong wake. But no. This was a send-off for John Kelly from Derry, who turned out to be the reinvented John Cushnan from Belfast. They were one and the same man. To the people at the wake, Kelly was a single man with no family background to speak of. As Kelly, he could blend in easily with the Irish community in Clapham: Kelly is one of the most common Irish surnames in the world along with Murphy and O'Sullivan. As Cushnan he would have stuck out like a sore thumb. He must have made up his mind not only to vanish completely from our lives but also to disguise his back story for as long as he could. It was an intelligent move on his part to go under the radar and avoid irritating and awkward questions from his new community.

As I studied the individual items on my desk in 2013, I cursed myself for not investigating his twenty-two 'missing' years sooner. Had I started immediately, in 1982, I would have been able to track down a lot of his friends from the Clapham days. It would have been a slog in that pre-internet, pre-Google age but in many ways it would have been easier. Alas, it wasn't until thirty years later that I got the kick-start to try to piece together the jigsaw. A combination of having time on my hands, the death of my mother in 2011 and a series of serendipitous and encouraging encounters conspired to prompt me to get the blue folder out.

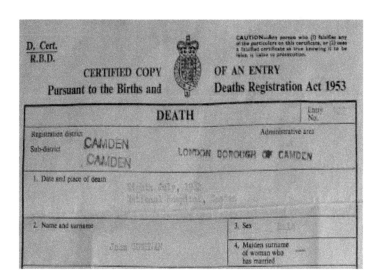

My father's death certificate

In addition to the contents of the blue folder, I had a copy of my father's death certificate. I had forgotten that I was the 'informant', as they call it. I got the year of his birth wrong. It is recorded on the certificate as 11th February 1924. He was born on 11th February 1925. It says in the signature box 'I certify that the particulars given by me above are true to the best of my knowledge and belief.' So I think I am in the clear.

The death certificate notes that my father lived in the London Borough of Camden. He died on 8th July 1982 in the National Hospital, London. His name is stated as John Cushnan and his given place of birth is Belfast, Northern Ireland. I guessed that he was still a tailor's cloth cutter; only later did I find out that he was a handyman for the Express Lift Company. So, two mistakes on the death certificate, but it was 'true to the best of my knowledge and belief'.

My father's address was a bedsit at 6 Orlando Road, Clapham Old Town. The cause of death was 'intracranial tumour'. The death certificate itself is dated 12th July 1982.

Ashton Funeral Services on South Side, Clapham Common, handled the arrangements. I should note right here that the funeral was paid for by Rose & Crown patrons (£661.60), with the lion's share contributed by landlord Jim Nicholson, a collective act that was a strong indicator that my father was both well known and well liked in his later years.

The funeral service took place on Monday 19th July 1982 in the beautiful St Mary's Roman Catholic Church on Clapham Park Road. Ashton's had planned a short additional service at Lambeth Cemetery chapel. Apart from the hearse, there were two cars to transport twelve mourners. The cortege left at 11.00 a.m. and the burial took place at 11.30 a.m.

During our short visit to Clapham, Kevin and I had an opportunity to see my father's bedsit, which was on the top floor of a large house. I think of him hauling himself up the stairs after a night on the tiles. It was one room about the size of a standard hotel room. He shared a bathroom and toilet with other residents. At the time, or on the journey back, I scribbled some notes to remind me of what he left behind.

The room had a high double bed. There was a small mahogany or teak dresser and a narrow wardrobe. The dull carpet had threadbare patches. There was a large bowl and a jug, presumably for a quick wash or shave. On the wall above the bowl hung a small mirror. There was a one- or two-ring electric stove. Soon after I got home, I turned my memory into a poem called 'Bedsit':

This was it, his bedsit,
his bowl of used Bic razors donated by friends,
his one pot, one pan, kettle and mug,
his belongings that would fill half a pillowcase,
his last years in this eight by ten room,
a testimony to his miserable life,
punishment of sorts
for abandoning seven kids and a wife.

It's not a great poem, but it records things that were important to me at the time. The Bic disposable razors stick in my mind as a symbol of how far he had fallen. My father relied on near-blunt shaving equipment from his pals. Even today, when I see Bic multi-packs in shops, I remember that bedsit. It really was a miserable room. No wonder he spent as much time out of it as he could.

The blue folder contained a letter from the Express Lift Company advising my father that it owed him a productivity payment of £79.50. I requested the money and it arrived in a brown payment-slip envelope. I sent it home

to my mother in Belfast. It was the first money she had
received from my father in over two decades.

From the funeral's floral bouquets there were eight
sympathy cards. They were from 'friends and management
of the Nestle company', 'RNA (Royal Naval Association)
Battersea', 'managers and fellow workers at the Express
Lift Company', 'pals George, Alf & Dennis', Judy & Vin',

'Alf, Jim & Doug', 'Helen & Denize' (with a zed), and 'friends at the Rose & Crown'.

There is a mass card from Judy & Vin on which their surname, McManus, is included. It reads: 'The Holy Sacrifice of the Mass will be offered for the repose of the soul of John Cushion [sic]'. It is one of the banes of my life that so many people don't spell Cushnan correctly, even when it is written or typed clearly or when it is spelled out slowly on the phone. 'Cushion' is the most common misspelling of our name after 'Cushman'. (I have also encountered Cushner, Kushner, Krushner, Cushan, Cusson and Cashin. A long time ago the name was Cushnahan but time squeezed two letters out of it.) No such complications with the more straightforward 'Kelly', though!

The blue folder also contained five associate membership cards dating from 1973 to 1977 for The Royal British

Legion Club in Clapham. They all refer to 'Kelly' – either 'J. Kelly' or 'R. J. Kelly'. I have no idea what the R stood for – runaway? From the receipts, annual membership ranged from 55p to 75p. The real incentive for an associate member was discounted alcohol. The Royal British Legion is an organisation committed to the welfare of the British Armed Forces, veterans and their families. *Committed to the welfare of families.* I wonder if my father, drinking his cut-price stout and rum, ever realised what a hypocrite he was. Family? What family? I've no family. I'm a single man. From Derry. Kelly's the name. Cheers!

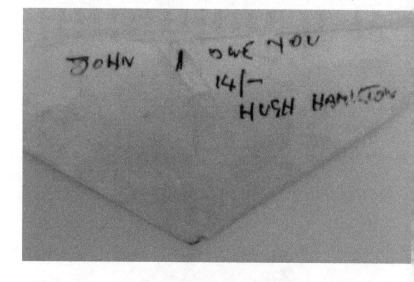

Among the bits and pieces in the blue folder is the lip of an envelope on which Hugh Hamilton, club secretary at the British Legion, had scrawled 'John, I owe you 14 shillings'. Whatever that was about, it probably sounded like a windfall to my father. For comparison, fourteen shillings is about ten pounds in today's money. At the time, it would have bought about five pints of beer. Drinks all round, no doubt. The most interesting thing about this scrap of paper, though, is the currency. The United Kingdom changed from pounds, shillings and pence to decimal currency on 15 February 1971. So, the note suggests that my father was living in Clapham before 1971. It's a small but important detail, at least to me. It seems that he lived in the area for at least twelve years, from 1970 to his death in 1982.

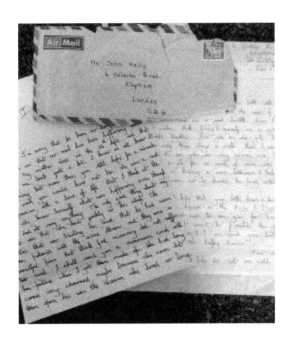

In the blue folder were two letters, both from a couple called Liz and Gerry. Frustratingly, I do not have their surnames. One of the letters is dated 23rd October 1981; the other, 1st December with no specified year. They were sent by airmail from an address in Grattan Park, Greystones, Co. Wicklow, Ireland, to my father at Orlando Road. Here's the October one:

Dear John,

I'm sorry that it's been so long since you've heard from us. But so much has been happening since we saw you. My mother died on the 26th September and that has set me back quite a lot. I know we all knew it was coming but even then you still hope for a miracle. I only wish you could have met her. She was a real jolly person with a love of life. But I think at the end she knew herself what was happening even though she didn't say anything. The only good thing about any of it was that she died peacefully in her sleep. The doctor that was treating her said that he had seen other patients with the same illness and they were in dreadful pain. But thank God Mammy did not suffer too much. I shall send you a memoriam card with her picture when I get them made up. She had lung cancer, very advanced. Maybe because she never let them open her was the reason she lived so long.

Well, I think we should talk on a more cheerful note now. How are you keeping, John? I do hope well. I want you to give my love to George especially and tell him Gerry was asking for him. Then tell Alfie and Eddie and big John and the rest of the lads, we send our best wishes. Hope they are all well and in good health. Please also convey our best wishes to Jim [the boss]. I hope you're looking after yourself and eating all you can. When we come back in the New Year for a few days, we want to see an improved Kelly. So be warned. We will arrive some night into the Rose & Crown and surprise you!

Both Gerry and I were very sad to leave you all behind us but things never work out the way we would all like. The night we left London, I guess all our nerves were a little on edge. Gerry was a bit hard on you that night but he never meant any harm. He's very fond of you really and so also am I. But I think he was thinking ahead to all the trouble there was going to be with Cleo and all her family. So, if either of us said anything out of turn, then you'll have to forgive us both. The only thing about that night that I can remember is that I was sick going on the boat. But then I was so worked up with all I had to face that I'm not surprised I felt sick.

But now that we're here, it isn't as bad as we thought. Cleo has said that she will give Gerry the divorce and she will sign any papers that need signing. They have come to an agreement about him maintaining the baby. So, we hope to be over to London in the New Year to start the legal proceedings, and then we'll drop in on you. But I know it will be our secret why the two of us go over. I don't mind George knowing as I trust George to be a trustworthy person. Well, I guess that's all the news about Gerry and I in regards to his divorce but if there are any changes, I'll let you know.

Well John, what have you been doing. I hope you are working hard. Both Gerry and myself are looking for a job but no luck yet. So, let's hope that we'll get something soon, at least coming up to Christmas. It's only a short time to go until Christmas. At least we have my own home to stay in until we get on our feet. That helps us a lot and we have no rent to worry about. What sort of a holiday did George and Alfie have? I hope they had a good time. Both Gerry and myself went away for a few days around Ireland just after we came home from London. I guess he wanted to try out the new car. So, we started out from Galway and stopped off in Cork, Killarney and Limerick where we passed through Listowel during their racing week. We stayed one night in Ballybunion and then drove back up through Waterford, Wexford and Wicklow. We even passed through Alfie's home town Fermoy which is a lovely little spot. Well, I guess that's all the news for now. So, until you hear from me again, take care and look after yourself. Give George our best wishes and hope to see you all soon.

Love and best wishes, Liz & Gerry
XXX'

The thing that strikes me about this letter is the love and
friendship that emanates from Liz who wrote it. She cares
for my father ('I hope you're looking after yourself and
eating all you can'; 'We want to see an improved Kelly.')
The mention of Gerry being a bit hard on my father but 'he
never meant any harm', talk of nerves on edge, the tension
of a divorce from Cleo, which involved a baby: 'it will be
our secret' make me wonder whether my father was tangled
up in some kind of affair or if he was just a friendly
onlooker. I can't help reading between the lines, but it's
nothing other speculation on my part. Still, the letter
expresses a genuine fondness for my father. He clearly had
friends and, on the strength of this letter and other sources,
they were good friends, some close and protective of him.
He left us and found them, and that probably made his self-
imposed exile a little more comfortable and secure.

I have wondered when it became clear to the Rose &
Crown clientele that his surname was Cushnan, not Kelly,
and what the reaction was. It could well be that others in
his circle had also changed their names; the Irish 'club' was
like a secret society. 'Whatever you say, say nothing.'
Omertà. It's impossible to say how long it took him to
settle into his new Irish community and whether or not he
felt homesick, but settle in he eventually did.

The second letter, dated 1st December, is also addressed
to 'George'. I have since found out that George, or
'Scottish George' as he was known, was one of my father's
closest friends.

Dear John and George,

I hope that you are both well and not working too hard. I hope also that all the rest of the lads in the Rose & Crown are in good health. Give them all our best wishes. Both Gerry and myself are in good health and still together. I've got my old job back in Bray but only three days a week. But I was glad to take it as jobs are very scarce over here. Gerry is doing a job for an aunt of mine who lives in Dublin. She is having a new bathroom and toilet built onto the house, so he should be busy until Christmas.

Well lads, I hope that you both have a lovely Christmas and don't *drown* in the Rose & Crown. I wish we could get over to see you for Christmas but I'm afraid that it won't be possible this year. So, on behalf of Gerry and I, we wish you both a good and peaceful and happy Christmas.

How is the weather over there? I hope it's not as cold as it is here. I wish we had a mild climate in winter and a very nice hot summer.

But I'm afraid that Ireland is a nice place to live except for its cold and wet Winters.

I hope you have all your Christmas lists ready for Santa Claus, as it's best to get in first. I've sent mine away but I'm doubtful if Santa will bring me what I want, (Frank Sinatra with a red ribbon tied under his chin). Mind you, I'll make do with a County Down house as a last resort.

I'm afraid that each year everything just seems to go up in price, except the wages to meet the costs. So, both Gerry and myself are thinking of doing a bank, Bonnie & Clyde style. So, if you don't hear from us after Christmas, you'll have to send a cake with a file. But maybe our sweeps ticket might come up in January and then we'll be straight over to Jim and the Rose & Crown, and buy you all a drink. Take care and look after yourselves.

Love and best wishes, Liz and Gerry XXX

This letter is less chatty than the first one, and seems to be more in the vein of keeping in touch. The most intriguing line is 'both Gerry and myself are in good health *and still together*' (my emphasis). There is definitely another story going on among friends. I wonder if, when my father read those two letters from Ireland, he ever sat back and thought about Belfast and what he had left behind. I wonder, too, if he ever considered moving back to Ireland, not to us but to 'home turf'. I know he had no interest in his family in Belfast, but Ireland always has a pull for the Irish. Being one of the Clapham Irish was as far as he got.

The Social Security correspondence, dated 12 July 1982, requested information from John in order to avoid delays in payment of benefits. My father had obviously not got round to filling it in before he died. The letter contains his National Insurance number, offering a tantalising key to his employment records and movements but, alas, due to officialdom's confidentiality rules, even for a person long dead, my hopes of uncovering any facts were dashed.

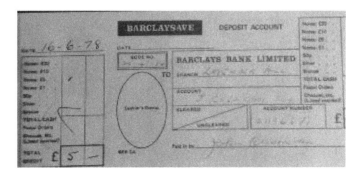

The cheque book – Barclay's Bank, Lavender Hill branch, Wandsworth Road – is unused. The paying-in book has an entry – a deposit of £5 – and my father's neat signature. I made enquiries at the bank. An administrative assistant wrote back: 'Unfortunately, we have been unable to locate any record of [the accounts] using the information available. As records are kept open indefinitely on inactive dormant accounts, and information of closed accounts is maintained for up to six years, we can only conclude the accounts you have enquired about were previously closed following the withdrawal of funds.' So, the account had been closed down many years ago because of inactivity, and there was no money in it anyway.

But at least I have my father's autograph! Note it is John *Cushnan*.

There were nine photographs in the folder:

- a man standing by what could be an olive tree;
- three women, all smoking, sitting in a horse-drawn carriage;
- two women posing at the front door of a house;
- a man swimming in the sea;
- a man (the swimmer) having a drink on a hotel balcony;
- the swimmer, two elderly women and my father posing outside in the sun;
- a bride, a groom and four others standing by a church door;
- a passport-size photograph of a young boy of maybe five or six years old;
- a passport-size photograph of a woman in her forties (my best guess).

I'll talk about them a bit more in Chapter 8.

My father's old, battered leather wallet

Finally, in this array of miscellaneous items was my father's brown leather wallet. It was well-worn and ripped along one seam. It smelled musty but I could also detect a mixture of leather and nicotine. The wallet was probably empty most of the time during my father's twenty-two 'missing' years.

The blue folder was a scruffy old thing back in 1982 and it has since fallen apart and been binned. I have a small regret about throwing it away because, useless though it was as a folder, it was still one of his possessions, his personal filing system.

It occurred to me that there was no passport. Perhaps he didn't own one, but there are a couple of indications that he may have gone on holiday to Greece or Spain with friends, in which case a passport would have been necessary. I am convinced that some of my father's possessions were, let's say, 'acquired' by the friends who sorted out his bedsit. He didn't have much but surely he had more that the ragbag contents of that blue folder. There wasn't even a copper coin. Whoever disposed of his clothes and shoes would have had the pick of anything valuable or useful. Perhaps I'm being unfair. Whatever really happened, all we knew of him were the exhibits described above.

Earlier on I said that my father pretty much vanished in 1960. It's true that he never returned to our family home, but he did surface around eighteen months later after being summoned by social services to appear at Lisburn Petty Sessions Court charged with a failure to pay child support. My sister Sheila spoke to my Aunt Sheila, my mother's sister, about the memory, a particularly stressful and embarrassing episode for my mother. My father had been found guilty of neglect and fined £5, which he promptly pulled out of his coat pocket and cockily handed over to the magistrate. He was ordered to pay my mother £6.6.0. He requested time with the children. The oldest, Paul (12), wouldn't talk to him; Sean (11) did. My sister Sheila, around 5 at the time, has a vague memory of him giving her and brother Kevin (3) a box of Smarties each. But after that court case he really did vanish.

I have been reading various articles about family break-ups in this modern era where there is a growing tendency to share experiences with the wider public, particularly via social media. The urge to offload on Facebook and Twitter seems to be contagious. In 1960, family traumas such as separating parents, were private affairs with only a few close relatives allowed into the secret. There was shame and embarrassment, and it was none of anyone else's business. Today's advice to separating parents – avoid drowning in misery, keep children in the loop about what is going on, emphasise that the split is not the children's fault and so on – would have been unthinkable sixty years ago.

My mother never displayed any misery. She got on with being a busy single parent. She never talked to us about why our father left and we never asked. She didn't have to reassure us that we were not to blame because we knew that anyway; most of us were far too young at the time to be traumatised or affected by the fallout.

In 2018, as I write this memoir, there is a plethora of advice available about the effects of dramatic incidents on a child's life and their ability to deal with negative things. My attitude to my father's leaving is much the same now as it was then – indifference and ambivalence. I was a timid child right through to my teens and I have always been apprehensive and nervous in the company of strangers. I cannot help but wonder: if my father had stayed with us, would I have been less timid? Would his presence have toughened me up in some way? Might he have changed my personality and the choices I made as an adult? How influential would he have been? Would I be more sporty? Would I be more confident? Would I be less reliable? Less trustworthy? The speculation never stops.

If he had lived, my father would have been well into his nineties by the time I started to investigate his life in 2013 and, with the passage of so much time, most of his friends were dead and gone. But all was not lost.

I wrote to the address at Greystones, Co. Wicklow, the address given by Liz and Gerry, the couple who sent the two airmail letters from Ireland. It turned out Liz and Gerry's daughter still lived in the house and she was able to tell me that Liz and Gerry had moved to the Costa Blanca in 2001.

On 3 July 2015 I got a phone call from Gerry who said he would try to help me as much as his memory would allow.

He told me that he always knew my father as John Kelly from Derry and that he never heard about any family in Belfast. Gerry only became aware of the Cushnan name after my father died. He was, he said, very surprised as they had been the closest of friends. Gerry never had any reason to suspect that my father was anything other than he was. (Had my father never let anything slip in a drunken conversation, I thought. Did nobody twig? Was no one suspicious about this man with no real background?) Gerry thought my father worked for the Express Lift Company, perhaps as a handyman, in and around London. He was apparently a hard worker, happy enough to do overtime for extra cash, but he was pretty hopeless with money. In those days, many workers were paid in cash on a Friday. My father would leave work with a bunch of mates and go straight to the pub, usually the Rose & Crown, and drink a fair amount of his wages. On Saturday mornings he would hit the bookies with whatever money he had left, and, it seems, he was more unlucky than lucky. By Saturday evening he would be skint. Gerry said he got into the habit of taking 'a few quid' out of my father's wallet on Friday nights to give back to him on Saturday afternoons. What with booze, betting and cigarettes, there wasn't much left for food and other essentials. Liz and Gerry frequently took my father home to give him dinner because they worried he was not eating enough. Five days out of seven each week my father didn't have the means to stock up on groceries. I wondered whether there were ever any problems with his bedsit landlord if he couldn't stump up the rent. It seems likely, although his circle of friends might have rallied round when times got tough.

Gerry finished the phone call by saying, 'John was a good man. I liked him very much.' Up to that point, I had not heard anyone talk about my father in anything other than negative and critical terms. It seems that, with friends like Liz and Gerry, he was fortunate to have people who cared enough to look after him. He had unburdened himself of parental responsibilities and could choose to be whoever he wanted to be. He had made a new life for himself, becoming a loveable Irish charmer who mixed with other Irish charmers.

I am conscious, as I write about him, that I keep referring to him as 'my father', not Dad, Daddy or any other term of endearment. At this stage in the story, I feel it is better to keep him at arm's length.

Gerry's phone call was helpful in various ways, not least in confirming that my father earned his money through hard graft but usually frittered it away within forty-eight hours of being handed his pay packet. It's not out of the question that the main reason he left Belfast, or was told to leave by my exasperated mother, was to do with money or lack of it to support the household. Alcohol-fuelled aggression at home may well have added to tensions in the relationship, things I would not have paid much attention to at the age of six.

CHAPTER 3: Fathers and Sons

This investigation into my missing father is not a misery memoir. It's not some boo-hoo story, a 'poor-little-Joe' tale. This memoir does not rest on any notion that my life has been ruined or adversely affected by my father's abandonment. I don't carry any visible or mental scars and I haven't experienced muscle strain from dragging a ton of heavy baggage with me from the past.

As I was growing up, I was used to having one parent, and not having another one around didn't bother me at all. The only time I thought about my father was when I saw my friends' fathers collecting them from school, or playing 'dads and lads' football, or helping to build guiders (death-trap contraptions made from wood, pram wheels and rope) or teaching them to ride bikes. My brother Paul, particularly, was a sucker for sentimental songs like 'Nobody's Child' (Hank Snow), 'My Son Calls Another Man Daddy' (Hank Williams), 'Daddy Don't You Walk So Fast' (Daniel Boone), and 'Don't Cry Daddy' (Elvis Presley). It never occurred to me at the time to make any kind of connection between our fatherless family and the sentimental sadness of heartstring-tuggers like these. They were just songs, irrelevant to the way we lived.

Much later in life at a job interview when I was answering a question about my upbringing, the interviewer asked if I ever felt disadvantaged by not having a father present in my formative years. Quick as a flash, I answered no. The quick-as-a-flash response was both instinctive and accurate. My mother stepped up and singlehandedly took care of her kids' welfare and all the other stuff involved in raising a family. If I really thought about it during my development, I might well have asked: 'Who needs a father anyway?'

As I have been researching my own story, I have tried to figure out what a great father might look like and to assess what I might have missed, assuming my own father was a good, decent, kindly man. Here's what I've come up with after a great deal of reading and thought.

A good father is a steady provider who works to see that his family has the necessities of life. He does everything in his power to keep his family safe physically, emotionally and spiritually. He shares his knowledge and principles to help his children grow and develop, and shows them kindness and compassion. He sets a good example for his children and he is revered by them for his moral character and actions. Of course, he shares these responsibilities with his wife or partner, to whom he is totally faithful. Therefore, he is a protector, teacher, friend, exemplar, patriarch, disciplinarian, spiritual leader and devoted partner – a good man, a good husband, a good father.

When I was growing up, I gleaned a great deal of knowledge about fathers from Westerns and from fiction, fathers like Atticus Finch in *To Kill A Mockingbird*, Ben Cartwright in *Bonanza*, Big John Cannon in *The High Chaparral*, Joseph 'Rocky' Rockford in *The Rockford Files*, even Fred Flintstone. My sister Sheila once described me as 'odd'. She might be right! Closer to home, I had big brothers, cousins and uncles that I looked up to, as a kid does, and I got through whatever was happening around me. But even now, when I'm in my sixties, I wonder what might have happened had my father not walked out. Would I be a different man? Would I have had the same interests? Would I have had the same career? Would our home have been a happy one? (It was without him.) Would I have been able to cast a fishing line? Would I have followed my father's example and become a heavy smoker, a heavy drinker, a gambler?

I have had two fathers in my life. My biological father who vanished and my father-in-law Jack. I knew Jack for thirty-four years. He died in 2011, the same year my mother passed away. Jack was an adventurous and gifted man in many ways. Way back before I knew him, in the days before cheap flights and holiday package deals, he would hitch up a caravan and drive his wife and two young children from Middlesbrough to the Algarve or the south of France and other distant places. He loved his family holidays. He was practical too. He built tables, cabinets and other furniture. He constructed a toy cooker, with amazing detail, for one of my sons. He was a very keen musician and once took it upon himself to buy a self-assembly organ. When it arrived, he was a little taken aback because all the instructions were in German. Undeterred, he translated the odd word here and there, followed the diagrams and before long he was belting out show tunes. He was a low handicap golfer and a decent painter. Some of his work still hangs on our walls. He is probably the best 'father' role model I have encountered in my lifetime.

Of course, we can't choose our parents; mums and dads mean different things to different people. I know many people who adore their fathers and others who have difficulty with their relationships. Celebrity autobiographies and biographies are a rich source of different types of paternal relationships. In June 2018, the *Sunday Times* ran a piece about the Conservative politician David Davis. In the late 1940s, his father, a married man, had an affair with his mother who became pregnant; his father subsequently abandoned the relationship to remain with his wife. Davis tracked his father down many years later and they spent a couple of hours talking in a pub. 'I liked him. He was a charming man,' Davis wrote. It was the one and only time father and son met. His father explained that he had a family of his own now and he didn't want to disrupt it with any shocking revelations about the past. Davis never tried to contact his father again and had no idea if he was still alive. So much of this story struck home, especially the father just walking away from any and all responsibility and choosing never to play any part in his son's life. [6]

The Northern Irish radio and television presenter Gerry Kelly (not to be confused with the Sinn Fein politician of the same name) writes about his father in his memoir *Kelly* (published 2008). I was struck by the similarities between his family story and ours. He writes:

> Life in the Kelly household was soon to be turned on its head when, in the early sixties, my father left the family home on the pretext of going to Scotland to work. Whether he did find employment or not, no one knows, because we never heard from him again. He literally abandoned his wife and five children without a single thought as to how we would survive.[7]

[6] https://www.thetimes.co.uk/article/david-davis-tells-of-tracking-down-father-to-meet-just-once-kcmr5rjft

[7] Gerry Kelly, *Kelly, A Memoir*, with Don Anderson, page 10, (Gill & Macmillan, 2008)

Gerry's father was an alcoholic and he recalls many rows between his parents. Booze played a significant part in my father's life too, and like Gerry, I don't think I will ever forgive my father for abandoning us. But unlike me, Gerry never had any inclination to find out what happened to his father. 'As far as I am concerned, my father died when I was 10 years old,' Gerry writes.[8]

In his 2014 family memoir *Not My Father's Son*, Scottish-born actor Alan Cumming makes a very interesting point:

> Memory is so subjective. We all remember in a visceral, emotional way, and so even if we agree on the facts – what was said, what happened where and when, what we take away and store from a moment, what we feel about it can vary radically.[9]

I understand what he means, especially when you're trying to recall and describe the distant past. Cumming's childhood was ruined by his father's anger and rage, and the dreadful experiences he endured cast a long, dark shadow into adulthood. When asked why he decided to write the book, Cumming said he wanted to expunge a horrible series of events from his psyche. But later, in a television interview, he concluded that he needed to

---

[8] Gerry Kelly, *Kelly, A Memoir*, with Don Anderson, page 11, (Gill & Macmillan, 2008)
[9] Alan Cumming, *Not My Father's Son* (Canongate, 2014)

embrace his father's memory, as father and son are inextricably connected biologically if not emotionally. In the memoir's acknowledgements, surprisingly, Cumming writes this: 'The next person I should thank is my father. Thank you, Alex Cumming, for siring me and ensuring I have lots of source material. I forgive you.' The power and courage of those last three words can only be understood by people who have read *Not My Father's Son*. Alan Cumming's story differs from mine by a wide margin, but I can't bring myself to exonerate or embrace my father's memory. I just can't. Cumming is a bigger man than me.

One of the intriguing things that comes out of a lot of these celebrity stories is that however tough their upbringing, the kids aren't necessarily scarred for life or disadvantaged in any way if they 'lose' a parent. In fact, it often seems like the reverse: trauma often lights a fuse and fuels determination.

On the flip side, there are many examples of fathers who were and are adored. Hugh Jackman describes his father, Chris, as his rock from whom he learned everything about loyalty and dependability, being there day in, day out, no matter what. Jackman's mother was the one who walked away from her husband and children, leaving the family's Australian home to travel to England. She never came back, although the mother/son relationship was rekindled in later years. Jackman gave some very good advice: 'You can't go through life obsessing about what might have been.'[10]

---

[10] https://www.news.com.au/entertainment/celebrity-life/the-painful-day-hugh-jackmans-mum-walked-out-on-him/news-story/283b5cff8939462b013e22f28d4ed9bf?from=public_rss

Formula One champion Jenson Button wrote beautifully and movingly about his late father, John, in the dedication to his 2017 autobiography, *Life To The Limit*:

> For the old boy. Simply put I couldn't have done any of it without you. Not just because you're my dad, who I love dearly but also because you were my best friend, my confidant and my inspiration then, now and forever. Together every step of the way, we made our dream a reality. I love you and I miss you.

The first time I read this tribute I felt envious that I couldn't write something similar about my father.

Barry McGuigan, the Northern Irish world featherweight champion boxer, wrote about his father in *Cyclone: My Story* (2011). His father died at the age of fifty-two in 1987.[11] 'When I think about my dad now, I remember him as just the loveliest guy: funny, witty, cultured, intelligent,' he writes. 'He was a very giving, very kind fellow, and fantastically talented too. He was always very good to me and was a great example for the way you should live your life: being a friend to people, being good, loyal and honourable.' This brought a lump to my throat too.

---

[11] Incidentally, McGuigan's father, Pat McGeegan (stage name) represented Ireland in the 1968 Eurovision Song Contest and came fourth with 'Chance of a Lifetime'.

The comedian and actor Bob Mortimer wrote in the *Daily Telegraph*:

> I didn't realise at the time how much the loss of my father would affect me. He died in a car crash when I was seven, leaving Mum to bring us up on her own. Until my mid-thirties, I thought that if you had to lose your dad, it would be good for it to happen early, but what my younger self didn't realise is that losing someone in that way really does affect you in all your relationships.

If I had lost my father through a car crash or other tragic accident, the trauma of that might well have affected my outlook on life and I have no idea how I would have coped with that. My father's decision to make his great escape quietly into the night carried no trauma or drama for me either at the time or at any point later.

Somewhere among the tangle of family love, frustration, emotions and moods sits *And When Did You Last See Your Father?* (1993) by the poet Blake Morrison. The book is excellent, even if it does try to kid us that Morrison remembered word-for-word conversations between him and his father from decades ago. At its core is a father and son love story, but not a smooth-running one by any means. It takes us from young Blake's anxious and, at times, humiliating teenage years growing up with a lively, domineering and adulterous father to an adult Blake who has to come to terms with his father's frailty. Adult Blake, a father in his own right, becomes witness to his own father's impending death. He wrestles with past memories and reassesses what he thinks the relationship with parents should be. As I read the book and, later, watched the film (released in 2007 starring Jim Broadbent and Colin Firth), I tried to imagine what my father would have been like in my teenage years. But it was impossible – he just didn't feature at all in my growing up – but it did make me wonder, as I have done numerous times, if I really did miss out on anything important, anything that would have made my life and my life choices better. And what if I had been there to hold my father's hand as he lay dying. What would I have said? What would he have said? On a scale of one to ten, how sad would I have felt?

In 2013, the *Daily Mail* ran an article with the headline: 'Growing up without a father can permanently alter the BRAIN (their capitals). Fatherless children are more likely to grow up angry and turn to drugs'. In the piece, Ben Spencer reflected on a research report by Dr Gabriella Gobbi and others from McGill University, Canada, which concluded that children brought up by a single mother have a higher risk of developing deviant behaviour, and that a home without a father could have greater impact on daughters than on sons. 'This is the first time research findings have shown that paternal deprivation during development affects the neurobiology of the offspring,' Spencer wrote.[12] As I read about the study I could not

_____

[12] Ben Spencer, 'Growing up without a father can permanently alter the BRAIN: Fatherless children are more likely to grow up angry and turn to drugs', *Daily Mail*, 4 December 2013.
https://www.dailymail.co.uk/sciencetech/article-2518247/Growing-father-permanently-alter-BRAIN-Fatherless-children-likely-grow-angry-turn-drugs.html

identify anything that was true in my own case. Perhaps this 2013 study has no relevance to fatherless households in the 1960s when I was growing up; modern family affairs may be different now. I have not grown up carrying anger with me about my absconding parent, nor have I turned to drugs. Nor have my sisters shown any inclination to deviance, although they did pinch my sweets one Christmas! I think it's dangerous to make generalisations such as this; not all children brought up by single mothers are at risk of becoming deviant in later life. But it's even more dangerous when you discover the basis on which the research was conducted. The McGill team came to their conclusions by studying mice, California mice to be precise; they claimed their findings had direct relevance to humans. There might be some truth somewhere in their findings, but it's certainly not true in my family's case.

My father went into a downward spiral where his interest in his family was superseded by his fondness for drinking and betting, both activities tantamount to pouring money down the drain. My mother's priorities were her children, maintaining a comfortable, happy home, and her Catholicism. She had no control over his money-wasting habits and she carried the constant burden of worry as to how much housekeeping money she would receive in any given week. She must have had many arguments with him over finances, frequently dealing with a drunk husband and witnessing over time her marriage drifting to a point of no return.

In 2001, Asda, the supermarket I worked for at the time, was beginning its second year of acquisition by the US behemoth Wal-Mart. I was sent to a Wal-Mart store in Festus, Missouri 'to see how stores should be run', as one American bigwig explained it rather pompously. My new buddy Steve, manager of the Festus outlet, drove me somewhere different for lunch each day – one day Chinese, another day burgers and one memorable trip was several miles away to a catfish restaurant, deep-fried and delicious – and on these trips along freeways and highways, I couldn't help but notice the endless billboards advertising, among other things, detective services. They posed the question: 'Who's your Daddy?', offered DNA paternity testing and displayed a phone number. I asked Steve if this was as big a problem as it seemed from the many billboards; he confirmed that it was a problem pretty much countrywide. He asked me about my family and I gave him a condensed version of the story. I looked at the billboards again – 'Who's YOUR Daddy?' and thought but didn't say out loud, 'I'm not sure I ever had one.'

Researching for this project, I posted questions and shared information on Facebook and Twitter in the hope that somebody somewhere would recognise a name, an incident or a photograph. Sometimes the responses were very helpful. Occasionally I would receive emails from people who had their own memories that they felt they wanted to share with me, and I am grateful for their contact. It is too easy to become engrossed in my own bubble and neglect to consider the experiences of others. The *Belfast Telegraph* kindly published several articles about my father and family, and one piece attracted responses.

One correspondent wrote:

> Thank you for sharing this article with us. It highlights a very important aspect of Irish life that has not been properly examined …

The choices facing your father haunted every male growing up in Belfast. The bleakness for Catholic men in particular was overwhelming, with the lack of work eroding the only signifier of manhood permitted in those days. For some men, their sense of loss of personal identity and self-worth was overwhelming. Drink eroded their judgement and offered an easy, if temporary, escape. Buddies in the bar and the bookies reinforced a false sense of acceptance and status, but failed to alleviate the pain of isolation and worthlessness. I grew up among them, but had the good fortune of having a teetotal father who had a job, six days a week for £6. Their despair was tangible and infectious. The subordinate status of Catholics just made the ensnarement complete for so many. Whenever I go back to Belfast I see the same patterns, except with younger and younger groups. Drugs have added to drink, and technology and designer clothes have become the new addictions, but with the same consequences. A culture where no one works cannot survive.

Another emailed:

> I read your article tonight … There is no doubt about it – times were hard. My father's cousin walked out on his wife and four children. He left with the woman down the street who left her children and then they settled in London. My grandmother married a man she never really loved but she was shy, an orphan, working in one of the stitching places and he helped her.

We are all a story as individuals and part of bigger stories.

As I trawled through newspaper and other archives, I noticed quite a few relationship stories and different reasons for and reactions to them. This one, from the Irish Independent in 2016 reported on John Herbert, 69, and his lifelong hope to find out what happened to his missing father, Peter. In 1957, Peter left England with a woman called Stella to travel to Ireland. He had embezzled money from a furniture company to help finance his high-rolling lifestyle, including the purchase of racehorses. John surmised that his father was a coward who had to run away. By running away, he left behind a wife and five young children. 'I am the first to accept that my father was not a nice or a good man. Despite his wrongdoings, I feel a son or daughter has a right to know about their father, especially his last resting place.' I do not know if John made any progress in his search. I empathise with him. Not knowing is a nagging irritation. As with my father, John is not under any illusions about his father's cowardice, selfishness or character. At least I know my father's last street address and his cemetery plot location.

But what about young Joe? What was his life like and how has it turned out? Well, I'll tell you.

CHAPTER 4: Joseph Gerard Patrick Cushnan

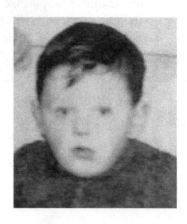

Me when I was three, 1957

This is me, Joseph Gerard Patrick Cushnan. That's a lot of names to carry around. 'Joseph Gerard' are my baptismal names and Patrick is the one acquired at my confirmation.

I was born on Sunday 10 January 1954 and raised to be a good Catholic. I loved the church, especially the showbiz side of it with mass and the fancy vestments and, if we were lucky, the stirring sermons. Most sermons were plodding endurance tests; many a pair of trousers ended up with shiny bottoms as we squirmed on the polished pews trying to alleviate the boredom.

Father Bernard McCann was the worst of them all. He was an older priest, and when he appeared out of the wings on a Sunday morning, I swear you could hear a collective sigh of resignation as the congregation braced itself for a long run. His sermons were excruciatingly slow; I remember the odd occasion when a snore would echo

50

around St Teresa's as someone grabbed the opportunity for forty winks.

Father McCann had an upstairs room in the priest's house on the Glen Road. He was in the habit of waiting for parishioners to walk past the house when he would open the window and shout: 'Hello. Can you get me ten greens (cigarettes) and drop them in on your way back. I'll drop a ten-bob note down to you.' A lot of people used to crouch down below the railings to keep out of his sight, but to no avail; he seemed to have been bestowed with in-built radar. He caught me a few times with a 'Hey boy' and, at ten years old, I couldn't think of an excuse to avoid the errand. He would get his cigarettes and his change, but never gave out any kind of gratuity in return.

Father Fred Hanson, however, was like Brian Blessed at loud volume. He delivered big booming talks that made everyone sit up and take notice. As I recall, he was the most internationally experienced priest in the parish and, therefore, his knowledge of the world and all its foibles far outweighed those of his less well-travelled colleagues. He was a no-nonsense sermon giver, a kind of bish-bash-bosh speaker who got to the point and wasted neither words nor time. He had a bit of an American twang to his voice and that made him more interesting and – nothing wrong with this at all – he was a big fan of Nana Mouskouri. If we were ever expecting him to visit us at home, an LP with the 'White Rose of Athens' on it was always on standby.

Services in church smelled of furniture polish and incense, and were punctuated by almost constant coughing from various parts of the congregation. I loved it all. I remember young missionary priests one time getting a round of applause after giving stirring, uplifting speeches. I had never heard applause in church before. As a kid it pumped me up. I even had semi-serious thoughts of becoming a priest myself, an ambition encouraged by a lot of Catholic mothers at the time. I recall dressing up as a priest, fashioning white toilet paper into a collar and mimicking that priestly way of talking with a lilt. I had a go at bellowing prayers like Father Fred.

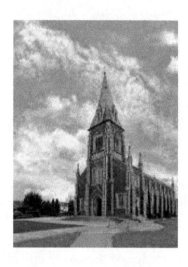

St Teresa's Church, Glen Road, Belfast

St Teresa's, built in 1911, was just across the Glen Road from our council flat in Bingnian Drive. The church is still there and has had a couple of facelifts and refurbishments over the years. I am still very fond of St. Teresa's; it played a big part in my life. I would often drop into the foyer and browse the little booklets, published by the Catholic Truth Society, offering advice and instruction on all sorts of religious matters, such as how to deal with doubting God, how to be a model Catholic and other nuggets of wisdom about life's journey and the power of faith and prayer.

I liked to light candles. There was a certain thrill at dropping a penny into a slot, taking a real candle, adjusting the wick, and lighting it from the flame of another candle before wedging it into a holder. Then you would stand for a couple of moments, head bowed in silent contemplation. More often, you adopted that stance so onlookers would marvel at the devotion of a wee lad. These days, a lot of churches use flame-free LED candles for health and safety reasons. I have no idea what God thinks about that, but I suppose it's the prayer that counts.

I loved the smell of incense; it was wonderfully sensuous and, dare I say, sexy. I always associate it with the Tantum Ergo, the Latin hymn which we would all sing with gusto without having a clue what it meant. My favourite hymn was 'Faith of Our Fathers', a rousing song that warned of dungeon, fire and sword – exciting and scary!

Every Sunday after mass, I would grab a bath towel when I got home, use it as a priest's cape and re-enact mass using our sideboard as an altar. I think I was tolerated by the rest of the family who just got used to Holy Joe's shenanigans. The treat for them was the communion bit when I served up white chocolate buttons. It was probably close to sacrilege, but no lightning bolt ever struck.

St Teresa's Church was close to, and associated with, St Teresa's Primary School, also still on the Glen Road. I started there in 1959 when I was five years old. I don't have many memories of those days but I do remember a favourite teacher, Mr (Gerry) Sadler. A few years into primary school, we were told to write about a journey of our choosing, local or exotic; it was up to us. I wrote a four- or five-page 'composition' about cycling down the Glen Road, joining the Falls Road, on my way to Smithfield Market in Belfast. It was almost certainly written in blue fountain pen ink (I didn't like Biros) and there weren't too many mistakes or blots. Mr Sadler read the essay, made a few marks and notes in red pen and said he liked the descriptions, the flow, the grammar and spelling, and gave me eight out of ten and a pat on the head. Even at that young age, I felt like a proper writer, a proven writer. Mr Sadler encouraged us to write anything we wanted and not just for school – limericks, poems about the Black Mountain at the back of our school, about trees, about the weather, about whatever was going on out in the streets of Belfast. With that kind of encouragement, I fell in love with the idea of being a writer. I was already a dreamer, so my imagination was fired up and ready to go. But just as life's little triumphs can lift you up, so its failures bring you back down to earth: my next essay was awarded five out of ten, I think; the one after that scraped a seven. I never bettered that eight, but no one can undo the fact that Mr Sadler liked *that* essay. In the end, I didn't become a writer – it's been no more than a hobby – but now that I'm in my sixties and retired, I'm trying to catch up with the ambition to become one.

Another memory makes my stomach churn even today. Warm milk. In my primary school days, pupils were given free milk, little third-of-a-pint bottles that sat outside in crates waiting for break time. In the winter, the milk would freeze making it impossible to drink, but worse, much, much worse, was the summer milk, which become warm in the sun. Those were the days of full fat milk, where a half inch of cream would form just under the foil bottle top. So not only did we have to drink the horrible, warm milk, but we also had to endure a blob of yucky cream before we could get to the liquid. Ghastly! We were told in no uncertain terms that if we wasted the milk, it would be a sinful insult to all the starving children in Africa. Mind games!

As I trawled old newspapers from the early sixties while doing some research for this memoir, I was struck by the prominent adverts for milk, portrayed as both a healthy and a trendy lifestyle drink. One ad showed two girls on bicycles, the blurb proclaiming that they were off to meet their boyfriends to have a glass of milk. Another pictured a woman scrubbing her doorstep 'before the neighbours see the dirt' with the promise of a glass of milk as a reward for all her hard graft. 'Sip it slowly,' she's advised. A third depicted a lovey-dovey couple drinking milk through straws to give them energy to go dancing. Those were the days when cigarette smoking was promoted as a sexy, romantic and stylish pastime, and kitchen appliances were believed to be suitable and practical gifts from husbands to wives. We've moved on apace!

Actually, mentioning Africa earlier stirs another memory, which will sound crass and ridiculous today. In our classroom there was a mechanical black puppet doll with an outstretched hand. In the centre of the hand was a slot rather like the coin trays on some supermarket trolleys. Every week we were encouraged to bring a big brown penny to school, place it in the doll's hand, pull a lever and watch the hand rise to the doll's mouth. When the doll swallowed the coin, we clapped: a good deed had been done. The money, we were told, was for charity – for the 'black babies'. There was nothing strange or outrageous about that in the 1960s. Today, we recoil in horror.

I have my first primary school report dated 31 December 1960, signed by F. H. McKenna, the head teacher, and Rita Cushnan, my mother. It was not a bad report. Everything was marked out of 10. I achieved 7 for sums, 10 for spelling, 8 for reading, 6 for handwriting and 8 for composition. Out of a class of forty-five, I came eighth. Pretty good. The only comment was the word 'Pass', which for 8 out of 45 was a bit mean. As far as I remember, my mother was very pleased with the report, but I wonder what my father would have said about it. He had walked out earlier that year. Somebody once asked me if the domestic upheaval affected my concentration. If the family had remained intact, would my examination marks have been higher? I doubt it as I was too young to understand much of the drama.

After primary school I went on to St Mary's Christian Brothers' Grammar School, situated further up the Glen Road. Some of the Christian Brothers seemed to relish corporal punishment, such as slaps to the hand with stiff leather straps or cuffs around the ear. There were rumours that some of the leather straps had coins sewn into the middle to ensure a painful whack. Looking back, it is tempting to say that such punishments did us little harm and taught us about discipline and honesty. But, actually, at times it was pretty brutal. I recall one of the teachers in particular, a 'civilian' called Mr Bennett who taught French. His penchant was for throwing things at us kids. If there was any whispering or irritating fidgeting or whatever, Mr Bennett would suddenly throw bits of chalk at the culprits or, worse, the blackboard duster, a solid block of wood. His strike rate was fairly impressive and one time he actually broke one boy's glasses. Getting hit on the head by a speeding bullet of chalk hurt, which may be why a lot of us had protective fringes. One thing we learned for sure was how to duck.

Me at 11, 1965

I also have my first report from that school. This report isn't so good – well, it's good in parts but a long way from distinguished. This time, subjects were marked out of 100, with 70 being a distinction, 55 a credit and 40 a pass. My marks were English 45; Latin 41; French 58; Irish 64; History 42; Geography 34; Arithmetic 47; Algebra 43; Geometry 25; Science 24; Drawing 42. Hmmm. A real mixed bag. Teacher comments included: 'Application to work satisfactory' and 'Progress – reasonably good but there is room for improvement'. I was neither brilliant nor a dunce. For a first year at 'big school', it was what it was. I did struggle to remember things and I was inclined to do the bare minimum homework. I was twelve years old in 1966 and my father, either en route to, or already in, London, would have been forty-one.[13]

---

[13] In fact, I hadn't read a novel or anything that could have been classed as a proper book. That came a little later, in my teens, when I read the

western *Shane* by Jack Schaefer. Westerns were, and still are, my passion. I attempted to read Dickens's *A Tale of Two Cities* because it was on the school curriculum but it bored me to tears and I stopped halfway through. Nowadays I devour books.

I left secondary school in 1970 with four GCE O-levels, English Language, Mathematics, French and Irish. I carried my educational underachievement like a millstone for the next decade and a half. I can't help but wonder, again, if my father had been present during my school years, and interested and involved, would I have been a better or worse student, or is that the best I could ever be? I can't imagine he would have helped with homework. I reckon his only reading material was a daily paper to study the racing form.

Twenty years after leaving school I finally balanced the books, so to speak. In 1992, I graduated with a BA Honours degree in social sciences from the Open University. At the time, studying with the OU was a struggle. When I started in 1987, my first son, David was three-years old and my second, Steven, was one. I was working in a fairly high-pressured job, getting up very early Monday to Friday to catch a commuter train from Hemel Hempstead to London and getting home after seven in the evenings. The thought of sitting down to study complex texts and writing assignments was a real chore, but I was determined to see it through. I studied aspects of social sciences, arts, economics, professional judgement and decision making – a varied selection but that's how the OU rolls. My wife Irene, my big sister Mary and my mum Rita came to my graduation ceremony at Newcastle City Hall. It was such a thrill to have my mum see her wee Joseph reach the giddy heights of a university degree.

I can't write about myself and not mention Westerns; they were a huge inspiration for me and played a major role in my education. My heroes both on the big screen and on television (Sunday afternoons!) included (in no particular order) John Wayne, James Stewart, Gary Cooper, Henry Fonda, Burt Lancaster, Robert Mitchum, Kirk Douglas, Gregory Peck, Charlton Heston, James Garner, Clint Eastwood and many more.

I was lucky enough to grow up during the golden era of TV Westerns – the late 1950s into the 1960s. Let me indulge in a little nostalgia; believe it or not, I have typed these names from memory! On the small screen, I enjoyed and learned much from:

Jock Mahoney (*The Range Rider*)

Clayton Moore and Jay Silverheels (Tonto) (*The Lone Ranger*)

William Bendix and Doug McClure (*Overland Trail*)

James Garner and Jack Kelly (*Maverick*)

James Arness, Dennis Weaver, Ken Curtis and Burt Reynolds (*Gunsmoke*)

Will Hutchins (*Tenderfoot/Sugarfoot*)

Chuck Connors (*The Rifleman*)

Ty Hardin (*Bronco*)

Clint Walker (*Cheyenne*)

Richard Boone (*Have Gun – Will Travel*)

Eric Fleming and Clint Eastwood (*Rawhide*)

John Smith and Robert Fuller (*Laramie*)

Lorne Greene, Michael Landon, Dan Blocker and Pernell Roberts (*Bonanza*)

Leif Erickson, Cameron Mitchell and Henry Darrow (*The High Chaparral*)

James Drury, Doug McClure and Lee J. Cobb (*The Virginian*)

Pete Duel and Ben Murphy (*Alias Smith and Jones*)

These shows were important in my formative years – they still are! – and just as important and influential as formal religion and education.

The Code of the West made as much sense to me as the Ten Commandments. Here's the gist of the Code:

- Live with humility and show respect
- Keep your word
- Do what you have to do and finish the job
- Be firm but fair
- Be loyal to your family and friends
- Be loyal to whoever pays you
- Believe in actions more than words
- Be mindful that not everything has a price
- Know when enough is enough
- Stand tall, be brave but watch your language

See what I mean? Darn good common sense.

Me, about 22 years old in the mid-1970s, not long after joining British Home Stores

On 17 September 1973, I joined British Home Stores as a trainee manager in Castle Place, Belfast. In those days, BHS was seen as the slightly poorer relation to the mighty Marks and Spencer, but still a force in its own right in fresh food, clothing and, particularly, lighting. I recall my first day walking nervously into the building in Castle Place. I was greeted by the Staff Manager, Arnette Martin, who introduced me briefly to the manager, Peter Gilbert, to be referred to as 'Mister Gilbert'. He referred to me as Mister Cushnan. When a new manager joined the store, he or she was presented to a gathering of all the store employees before opening time, and I was no exception. Mister Gilbert stood halfway up the stairs and welcomed me in front of all the staff; I had to join him on the stairs so that my new colleagues could give me a warm round of applause. Thank goodness I did not have to make a speech.

I was hired as a trainee manager and put on a nine-month training plan to give me a little experience of working in each section of the shop floor as well as areas behind the scenes, such as the stockroom and the cash office. I even had to do a stint learning how to bale cardboard for uplift and recycling.

Most of the managers were English and some were cocky, thinking that because they were on secondment from 'the mainland' (an expression that annoys me to this day), they were superior beings to us local guys. They thought it was hilarious to take the mickey out of our Belfast accents. The English managers lived in a company-owned house in Templepatrick, about ten miles outside of Belfast. This was a pretty dangerous time in Northern Ireland; in the wrong company, an English accent could spark violence. BHS Head Office shipped over a company car for the English managers to use, but when it arrived we were all surprised to see that it was a lovely shade of British army green. As soon as the penny dropped, the car was returned and a nice, shiny blue one was sent about a fortnight later. We locals laughed ourselves silly for a week or so.

One advantage of being located 'across the water' from Head Office was that we always received advance notice when the regional manager was due to visit. It gave us two days to ensure the store was looking its best. Mr Rathbone, of Falstaffian proportions, had a puffed-up ego and was fearsome. On the day of the visit, a number of us would scribble sales figures and percentages on the backs of our hands in case we were quizzed on how our departments were performing.

Around January 1974, after my nine-month training apprenticeship, I was appointed department manager of menswear and became the security coordinator. These were dark days in Belfast city centre, when barely a day went by without bomb scares and, sometimes, deafening explosions. Belfast stores employed security guards at entrances to search customers for incendiary devices and anything else threatening, and it was part of my job to look after this team. It was a pretty ineffective way to stop terrorists, but it was the done thing to give customers the impression that we were thinking about their safety. It brought a whole new dimension to customer care.

I remember a van exploding without warning outside the store in Castle Place. It was a massive blast on a busy Friday afternoon as I recall. The windows of our store and those of many other neighbouring buildings shattered, the impact sending blizzards of glass fragments up through the food hall. It was terrifying. We tended as best we could to the injured until ambulances arrived. Thankfully, none of the injuries were life-threatening. Glaziers boarded up the windows and made the shop as secure as possible. The store team stayed into the early hours of the following morning to sweep up and check every shelf and product to get the store ready to open as usual at nine o'clock on Saturday morning. It was always a matter of business as usual.

I remember a particularly nasty phase of incendiary devices being planted in city centre shops around Christmas, bringing worries about what might happen during the two days when shops were closed. A rota of shifts was devised, and I volunteered, along with another colleague, to stay in the store overnight on Boxing Day. Nothing happened from a security point of view, but it was spooky just being there. Every now and then drunks rapped the windows and shouted something obscene, even though they couldn't see us. At one point, one of the lifts suddenly sprung into life and both of us jumped out of our chairs. We checked it out but found nothing. It happened a couple more times that night but we just looked at each other and shrugged. If there was a ghost, we didn't see it.

I was at British Home Stores in Belfast from 1973 to February 1976, during what were probably the worst years of the Troubles. But it didn't just affect Belfast. People died or were injured all over Northern Ireland and in Great Britain. Here are just some of the incidents.

1973: In March, four car bombs planted by the IRA outside the Old Bailey in London caused multiple injuries. In May, five British soldiers were killed by an IRA bomb outside a hotel in Omagh. In June, six Protestant pensioners were killed and thirty-three others injured as a result of an IRA car bomb in Coleraine.

1974: In February, eight British soldiers were killed when an IRA bomb exploded on a coach travelling along the M62 in West Yorkshire. Also killed were the wife and two children of one of the deceased soldiers. In April, the Troubles claimed its 1,000th victim, a Fermanagh petrol station owner. In May, there were three UVF bombs in Dublin and one in Monaghan on the same day, killing thirty-three civilians and injuring around three hundred. In October, four British soldiers and a civilian were killed by IRA bombs in two pubs in Guildford. In November, a British soldier and a civilian were killed in an IRA explosion in a pub in Woolwich. In November, twenty-one civilians were killed when bombs exploded in two Birmingham pubs.

1975: In February, March and April, feuds erupted between rival paramilitary organisations on both sides resulting in many tit-for-tat assassinations. In July, four British soldiers were killed by an IRA bomb in County Armagh. In July, three members of the Miami Showband were killed by UVF gunmen posing as a border checkpoint military unit. Five people were killed by an IRA gun and bomb attack at a pub in Belfast. In August, the IRA exploded a bomb in a pub in Caterham, injuring thirty-three people, including ten soldiers. In September, five Protestants were killed and seven injured in a gun attack at an Orange Hall in County Armagh. Also in September, an IRA bomb exploded in the lobby of the London Hilton Hotel, killing two people and injuring sixty-three.

On and on it went – death, injury, destruction, worry and fear. These were the horrific times we lived through and yet it almost became a normal way of life. None of us could be certain that we would avoid surprise gun attacks or random explosions. At this time my father, in his late forties, would have been living in his Clapham bedsit, working, drinking and backing horses. During those years of death and destruction in Belfast, he never got in touch to see if we were safe. He must have had ice-cold water in his veins instead of blood. We could all have been blown to bits for all he knew or cared.

But troubled times though they were, there were lighter moments. During one of the many evacuations we endured following a telephoned bomb scare, the police and army brought a sniffer dog to roam the store in a bid to detect explosives. As the brave dog scrambled around and over the top of counter displays, it decided to stop on my department and do its business. After the all-clear, I had to grab a bin and shovel and scoop the poop before customers were allowed back in. Whenever anyone talks about rolling up their sleeves and getting their hands dirty, they are talking to an old campaigner here.

In my time at BHS Belfast, the darkest and saddest time for our family was the death of my brother Paul. He was twenty-five, married to Margaret, and had three young children, Paula, Jacqueline and Mark. When our father left us, Paul became the man of the house. For a time, he was a sheet metal worker, then a garage worker but he moved on to become a long-distance lorry driver to earn more money.

He made frequent ferry trips from Larne to Stranraer and Cairnryan in Scotland. On 6 December 1974 at around 11.15 p.m., he drove off the ferry at Cairnryan and took the A77 south before joining a short link road to the A75. Not far along this road – less than four miles from the ferry – near a farm called Inchparks, his lorry ended up in a ditch. In Belfast, in the early hours of the next morning, the police informed us of the accident. We were told that Paul had gone through the windscreen and landed face down in shallow water that was deep enough to drown him. We never found out what caused the accident. I was able to get a copy of his death certificate while researching this book, where it also mentions a depressed fracture of the skull. My brother Sean was the informant. He recorded our father's first name as Sean, although he was rarely known as such, I believe. Even more than four decades on, a shiver ran through me as I studied that certificate.

We were all devastated, especially my mother. Family and friends rallied round, as they do in tragic circumstances. Along with my cousins John Tierney and Tony Killen, I travelled by ferry to Cairnryan to identify Paul's body and complete any necessary paperwork. The identification procedure is pretty much how you see it in television dramas. When he was alive, Paul had a fringe. Lying dead on the table, his hair had been swept back. I nodded to confirm his identity and his face was re-covered. It was over in a matter of moments, some of the saddest moments of my life. I doubt my father had any inkling that his son had died. If he did know and didn't get in touch – well, that is unforgiveable.

I was twenty when Paul died. My most vivid recollection is from his time as a garage mechanic. He would come home from work smelling of oil and Swarfega, that magic green-gunge hand gel that cleans anything. He liked records, especially of Irish show bands and country music. One of his favourite songs was the Jim Reeves hit 'Blue Side of Lonesome'. He was also a fan of Irish singers like Joe Dolan and Dickie Rock, and he built up a decent collection of LPs and singles. I can picture some of the labels now – Pye, Emerald and Parlophone.

For a while Paul went through a phase of wearing a cravat instead of a tie. I recall other older boys sporting this fashion, so he wasn't out of place. But I associated cravats with P. G. Wodehouse characters and it certainly wasn't natural attire for Belfast. He also went through a phase for pipe smoking. He smoked cigarettes too but the pipe had some appeal, something to do with the style-and-swagger thing that teenagers go through perhaps. Once, when I was at home alone, I spotted his pipe on the hearth and thought I would have a go. After several attempts to get the thing lit, the tobacco took on a red glow and I sucked the life out of it. Oh dear! There's a method to pipe smoking and sucking is not part of it. All I was doing was ingesting horrible brown liquid. I spent hours being sick and it took ages for me to recover.[14]

Paul came to my rescue one time. I was walking down our street towards Benbradagh Gardens, not too far from home, when three or four bigger boys started to harass me – nothing violent, just pushing and shoving and getting in my way. I was a timid kid and this was one of those incidents that could have turned into a fight, especially if I'd uncharacteristically lashed out. I knew that if I ran away,

---

[14] In my early teens, I smoked for a week one summer. My friend Sean and I spent a week in a caravan on our own in Carnlough. We decided it was a good chance, unsupervised by adults, to practice a swaggering walk and smoking. We agreed on a brand – Peter Stuyvesant, American cigarettes – which we felt made us look like two stylish dudes. After our holiday, we went back home and never smoked again.

they would have chased me down. You know in those Superman films when all hope seems to be lost until *Whooooosh*, there he is? I kid you not, from out of nowhere, Paul and one of his mates appeared. Paul's boot connected with a boy's backside in an eye-watering kick and the bully-boys scattered. I was saved and he was the hero of the day. Looking after little brothers is part of what big brothers do.

Paul loved motorcycle racing and he took me to the Ulster Grand Prix at Dundrod a couple of times. His heroes in the 1960s were Giacomo Agostini, the Italian champion, our very own Tommy Robb, and Mike Hailwood and Phil Read from England. It was a thrilling spectacle and such an exciting noise as the bikes thundered past. His favoured position on the road circuit was the hairpin bend where there was a higher than average chance of high-speed skids and riders being thrown from their saddles. In those days there were no security restrictions, and spectators could just wander into and around the pits area, and Paul set himself the challenge of trying to blag baseball hats from the team crew members. He succeeded a few times, most notably acquiring a couple of Honda hats. The hats were particularly prized because they came from that faraway land, Japan. To us in Belfast, that was pretty exotic.

Paul's obsession with motorcycle racing was underscored by his purchase of a series of single records (45s) which were basically the sounds of bikes revving and racing with commentary by Murray Walker. He would play these endlessly and built up a pretty good knowledge of individual engine noises. For a time, Paul had a motorbike of his own. I think it was a 250cc Triumph or a BSA ('Best Scrap Available' was the joke). He didn't have it for long but he looked after it lovingly. A bike was not only a means of going fast, it had to gleam in the sunshine to impress people. My mother was not too keen on him owning a bike; I am pretty sure that as he rode off for a spin she was saying a couple of prayers for his safe return.

I also remember being with Paul and a couple of his mates on a car trip to the seaside. I can't recall where exactly where we went but I do remember us all singing along to Pat Boone's 'Love Letters in the Sand' on the radio as we approached a place to park. The performance was enough of a distraction to cause Paul to reverse into another vehicle. There was no damage, but a few heated words were exchanged with the vehicle's owner and then we got on with our day at the beach.

I accompanied him a couple of times when he drove his Hillman up a Black Mountain road to wash it using freezing water from a trough in a lay-by. He told me it wasn't ordinary water; it was mountain dew with added fly-squash remover. He sloshed the windscreen with a soaked sponge and, magically, the dead flies disappeared. I was impressed and wondered why he was trying not to smile at me.

My big brother Paul played a fundamental role in my formative years and was such an important ingredient in our one-parent family. I laughed at his silly jokes; I sang along with him as he belted out show band songs; I shared his joy when his children were born. And in the end I identified his body. That's an unbreakable bond right there.

After Paul's funeral, it was back to work because life goes on as we know it should. It was a sombre time for the family; they were dangerous times on Belfast's streets. But we always had our sense of humour to fall back on. I am reminded of something cheeky and childish that happened in BHS, Belfast.

Each afternoon, about an hour before the shop closed, the keyholder would come in and tour the building to start locking windows and fire doors to ensure a fully secure shut down when we all left for the evening. His tour took him down some stairs, around a corner and down a further flight to a fire door at the back of the store. One day, a couple of us disconnected a hand from one of the fashion department's mannequins and placed it on the handrail just around the corner of the stairwell. The keyholder almost jumped out of his skin when he touched the cold extremity. He was normally a gentle plodder as he did his rounds, but on that day, he bounded up the stairs and shot out on to the shop floor like a banshee with its tail on fire. We had decided in advance that if we had been identified as the culprits, our best defence rested on us arguing that we were only 'giving him a hand'. We screamed with laughter for ages afterwards, and he developed a suspicious eye in our company from that day on. It was daft things like that helped to counteract all the serious stuff going on around us.

Each place I worked in in Belfast employed people of different religions and backgrounds. At work, the banter was great. It really was a fun time. Then when the shop closed, usually at 5.30 p.m. (half day closing on Wednesdays), we would all go back home to our own 'territories'. At work we were friendly, helpful and funny; outside, we stepped back into a divided society.

A few times all buses were cancelled because of hijackings and riots and it was pretty scary to have to walk home up the Falls Road to the Glen Road, navigating a route past a blazing vehicle and choking on burning tyre smoke, hoping that soldiers and police didn't mistake me and other innocent commuters for troublemakers.

In February 1976, after three years in BHS Belfast, I moved to BHS Manchester. I was twenty-two. I said an emotional farewell to my mother and the rest of the family and headed to Aldergrove Airport, now Belfast International, for the flight to Manchester's Ringway Airport. After landing, I got a taxi to a pre-booked bed-and-breakfast in Stockport. It was the beginning of a new adventure, but I suffered from early pangs of homesickness, a feeling that took some time to fade. That first night I was a stranger in a strange land – indeed, a stranger with a strong Belfast accent in the strange land that was England.

My first day at BHS Oldham Street, Manchester, involved meeting the manager, Tony Steel, the deputy manager, Mary Clough, and the rest of the team. As with day one in Belfast, I was presented to all the store employees as the new boy and off I went to get to know my department, once again menswear.

Most of the department managers were women and not shy in playing tricks on this greenhorn in their midst. They tried to send me for buckets of steam, left-handed screwdrivers, glass hammers and other daft stuff, but I got the hang of their humour pretty quickly. Mary Clough warned me about a local gangster (I think his name was Wally) who was prone to use the store as a walk-through from Oldham Street to the other exit of the building. He and another big guy, his henchman-bodyguard would swagger through, looking mean and moody. Mary told me not to make eye contact or do anything to provoke a reaction. She didn't have to tell me twice. When they were in the store, I could feel menace in the air.

Tony Steel was a tall, handsome man and a lot of the female employees fancied him. But he had his moments. Frequently, Mary would rush around the shop floor warning us that Tony was on his way and he was 'on the turn'. Sure enough, he would appear with a sort of red mist about him. When he was in his bad moods he always found something wrong, but most of the time he was charming and helpful. When I became a store manager myself years later, I understood how many things could tick you off and swing your mood like Jekyll and Hyde. The pleasures and pain of retail management have to be experienced to understand who and what pushes the wrong buttons.

In my first weeks in Manchester, the company paid for my B&B expenses while I searched for a place to live. Half my lunch break was spent running down to the corner of Oldham Street to buy the first edition of the *Manchester Evening News* for the accommodation-to-let ads, then with a pocket full of coins, heading for the nearest phone box to ring to make appointments. I saw a lot of grim flats, bedsits and rooms in big houses. But eventually I found a flat off the Heaton Moor Road between Manchester and Stockport. My landlord was Mr Kola, a decent man, as I recall.

It was a small upstairs flat but big enough for one. It felt good to be in a place of my own rather than in the constrained environment of a guest house. But about six months later, my BHS colleague and pal Tom McGarrity, a Magherafelt man, was transferred to BHS in Stockport. So, we ended up getting a bigger place together on the Heaton Moor Road above some shops. Those were fun times. Tom helped me move my stuff from Lea Road, about a third of a mile away, and we did it all on foot, including carrying a heavy television set along the street. People must have thought we were bandits on a looting spree.

On the frequent occasions when my bus home from work arrived at the Heaton Moor bus stop coinciding with Tom's bus from Stockport, we would walk together to the flat. Between the bus stop and the flat were three pubs. It was

1976, a long hot summer, and a pint in each seemed to be appropriate (a pint of beer set you back a cool 21p).

We lived pretty much on takeaways and ale, and one memorable evening, 14th September 1976 to be precise (it was so memorable that I recorded it in a notebook) we went on a marathon pub crawl in Manchester taking in The Mitre Hotel, The Town Hall Tavern, The Vine Inn, The Crown, The Grey Horse, Flanagan's, The Portland Hotel, The Piccadilly Hotel and The Shakespeare. In one of the pubs, I have a clear memory of a woman sitting on a barstool drinking lager and blackcurrant and eating a beetroot sandwich. We got back to the flat in one piece, but next morning, we noticed a large glass ashtray on the table that had not been there before, and neither of us smoked. One of the pubs we often included in other jaunts was Tommy Duck's, a boozer like no other. It's long gone but it was famous for its collection of knickers pinned to the ceiling and for its coffin-shaped tables. We met Stephen Hancock there one evening, famous at the time as Ernie Bishop in Coronation Street. Tom kept insisting on calling him Ernie throughout. Ernie, er Stephen, was not amused but he remained polite.

In the Manchester store, I got used to people mimicking my Belfast accent. There was one so-called comedian, a blunt Northerner, who kept referring to me as 'on-the-run-Joe'. Someone stepped in after a while and told him in no uncertain terms to stop it. He tried to laugh it off, but he stopped after that. I must admit I was very conscious of my accent as there had been, and would continue to be, IRA atrocities in England. I tried to adopt a nondescript accent to disguise my roots. It was shameful and cowardly really, but tension was sometimes high, especially in the aftermath of an explosion.

But there was another reminder of the cultural and religious divisions prevalent back home. Two of the store's porters were from Ireland. Jimmy was a Protestant from Belfast and John was a Catholic from Dublin, and they were often at loggerheads. They despised each other but Jimmy had only one arm, which meant that he had to rely on John from time to time if some heavy lifting needed to be done. I got on all right with both of them, especially John who discovered my love of poetry and, every so often, would hand me a newspaper cutting containing a poem or an article about poetry. He was a great man to know.

Towards the end of 1976, BHS needed to cut costs at the Manchester store and they decided to remove at least one department manager – me. And so it came to pass that I was on the move again, this time to BHS Romford in Essex. I was sorry to leave Manchester and my buddy Tom, but that's the way it was in those days – young, single and transferable.

BHS Romford was fun, by and large, because us lowly managers had great camaraderie and a common sense of humour. We needed it because the store manager, Frank (but always Mr) Robinson, was old-school, and fierce, frightening and spooky in that he would suddenly appear out of nowhere and find something trivial worth two or three minutes of a bollocking. He had a sign on the wall behind his desk: 'What a wonderful day. Now watch some bastard ruin it.' He was so controlling that he even kept cleaning materials in a cupboard in his office. If I wanted a new cloth, I had to go the office, knock the door, wait for the invitation to enter and request the cloth. He would examine the old cloth and bark, 'There's a few more cleans left in that, son', and throw it back at me. He was not always particularly angry, but he pretended to be in order to maintain his authority, keeping us on our toes and in our places. In his own way, he taught all of us young managers a lot about retail management. He was a stickler for routines and details, and in retailing that is not a bad approach.

I shared a flat in Chadwell Heath, a short bus journey from Romford, with Richard Ashby who had a penchant for playing Ella Fitzgerald and Stevie Wonder LPs as often as he could. We would go to the local pub, The Cooper's Arms, to see a group called Ropey Boat who did a decent cover version of 'Love Potion Number 9', among other classics.

One of the assistant managers at Romford was someone to avoid at morning break time. He always ate the same thing: two crusty rolls filled with grated cheese and topped off with a spoonful of marmalade. The problem was that if you sat opposite him, he would talk non-stop while eating and it was a job to dodge sprays of his crusty crumbs. I can't remember a lot of the more important things in life but trivia seems to stick in my mind. For example, one of the bestselling items in BHS back in the day was a polo-necked jumper in various colours and I can still recall its item number (1530).

I met my wife Irene in BHS Romford. She transferred from Middlesbrough in 1977 to join as Assistant Staff Manager. Every morning, the management team would gather at men's underwear for a meeting to share Head Office mail and listen to any words of wisdom from the boss; it was there that our eyes met – a genuine 'brief' encounter! We married in 1980 and, nearly forty years on, we are still together.

I did holiday cover at various BHS stores in those years. At East Ham I was treated like royalty in the staff canteen at lunch time. Every day a plate would arrive with a mountain of food on it. For the first couple of days it was great – I loved it! – but gradually I began to dread it. Forcing food down when you're full is not recommended, but at the same time I didn't want to hurt the canteen manager's feelings by not eating it all. I was glad when the holiday fortnight was over. I didn't check the scales at home for a while.

Another holiday cover experience took me to BHS Hackney. On the first day, alarmingly, I was shown some baseball-type bats in cupboards near the front doors. Apparently it was a frequent occurrence for three or four thugs to swagger in and steal entire racks of clothing. The bats were meant to be a last resort if we needed to defend ourselves. However, the instruction from on high was not to put ourselves in harm's way. In my short spell at Hackney, the bats weren't used but at least three raids were made on the fashion department.

After a year in Romford, I was transferred to BHS Wood Green in North London, when I shared a flat in nearby Crouch End with my colleague and friend Paul Anderson, who arrived at Wood Green on the same day. I can't recall the landlord's name but he was a bulky Irishman in a Victor McLaglen kind of way. Our flat was above his office, very handy for nipping down each month to pay the rent and get our book stamped. We frequented a pub called The Stapleton Hall Tavern, just down the street. Some of its clientele were, shall we say, of dubious character. On our first visit, Paul and I were wearing trench coats as it was raining outside. To anybody shifty, we looked like policemen. There was much whispering and shuffling feet in the pub until we told them we were merely British Home Stores guys. One memorable customer always wore a leather cowboy hat and, from his swaying gait, appeared to be permanently tipsy. He would mooch around cadging drinks and cigarettes. We nicknamed him Buffalo Bill – but not to his face.

The flat above us was occupied by a tall Jamaican guy. We never knew his name but we exchanged greetings any time we saw each other. He had a habit, about once a week, of washing his car in the early hours of the morning to a high-volume soundtrack of reggae music. The language hurled at him from bedroom windows along the street was choice, but he didn't seem to care. When he was in residence, there was always a distinctive, sweet-smelling aroma on the stairwell. I wonder what that could have been?

My next flat-mate was David Christian who also worked at Wood Green, and we got on well too although we were quite different in some respects. David liked to look after his clothes and footwear whereas I was a bit more careless with my attire (sometimes I only ironed the front panels of my shirts!)

The camaraderie at Wood Green was as good as at Romford and we all often enjoyed a beer or three together after work in The Wellington across the road. BHS Wood Green was hard work but a lot of fun. The store manager was a bit of a stickler for merchandising standards via the morning and evening inspections and the two assistant managers were always trying to outdo each other to propel themselves to their next career promotion. The store manager wore hard-heeled shoes and had a distinctive rhythm to his footsteps. Sometimes, for fun, I would mimic his stride and walk up the corridor before sticking my head round the training room door to cries of 'You bastard!' from my colleagues.

In 1979, BHS changed from old NCR 'kerching' cash registers to new computerised IBM tills. The project was called 'Point of Sale Conversion'. I was chosen as one of six team leaders to implement training across the chain, starting in the Wood Green store. My new base, though, was Head Office. I remember feeling immensely proud when I walked into BHS Head Office on the Marylebone Road to start my new job. It was great fun but hard work during the new POS team's training on the new equipment. I enjoyed travelling to various UK locations, talking to groups of managers and staff about the exciting changes in the company. It was one of the most enjoyable phases of my career and I developed a hankering for a training job.

In 1984 I left BHS altogether. By that time I had been married for four years and our first son, David, was on his way. I joined Alfred Dunhill as administration manager in the jewellery division. The office was across the road from Fortnum and Mason, near Piccadilly Circus. It was a great area for spotting celebrities as they browsed the fancy shops. I saw Michael Caine, Terence Stamp, Adam Ant, and quite a few others over the years.

Dunhill hired an archivist to collect one of every luxury product they ever produced – lighters, cufflinks, writing instruments (pens and pencils to me and thee), etc., with a view to creating a small museum. In the old days, Dunhill shop managers were required to complete a daily diary of anything interesting. The archivist showed me a diary entry made in the mid-1950s that recorded a visit to the shop by Mr Laurel and Mr Hardy, and another some years earlier noting a visit by Douglas Fairbanks Jr. Senior royals from Buckingham Palace also liked to request a selection of items to peruse before deciding on a purchase; couriers were back and forth frequently.

From Dunhill I got a surprising opportunity to move to the Yorkshire Dales in 1987 to work as tourism and retail manager on the Duke of Devonshire's Bolton Abbey

Estate. It's a beautiful part of the world but the job was dull, not fully supported by the estate manager, and involved, with a few wonderful exceptions, a cast of very awkward characters not unlike some of the crotchety sorts in the TV series *All Creatures Great and Small*. While working at the estate, I got a personal tour of Chatsworth House by none other than the Duchess of Devonshire, a grand lady for sure, but very easy to talk to – knowledgeable and delightful company. Sadly (but also thankfully), the Bolton Abbey job was made redundant in 1989. The upside of the episode was that it got us out of the London area. We had a good time living in Skipton, a charming market town, and exploring some of the most amazing scenic locations.

After a short time, I joined Makro Self-Service Wholesalers in Kirkby, Liverpool, as an assistant general manager. Cue the removal van yet again and off we moved to Formby, near Southport. From Kirkby, I was promoted to general store manager, my first fully fledged senior management position, and transferred to Sheffield in 1991, then, in 1993, to Nottingham. I left Makro in 1995 after being head-hunted by Asda, which I left in 2005, and coasted with some freelance training and writing work. I was offered a job working as a retail manager for Frank Thomas, a motorcycle clothing company based in Northamptonshire. The job entailed lots of travelling around the UK, sometimes on pointless missions like a 200-mile drive for a one-hour shop visit. It wasn't a particularly efficient company and a lot of important decisions seemed to be made off the cuff. However, I did benefit from half a dozen trips to San Francisco to meet our US client, so it wasn't all bad. I was able to tick City Lights bookstore off my 'to do' list, where beat poets and writers like Allen Ginsberg and Charles Bukowski congregated in the 1960s to put the world to rights.

In 2007, I pretty much retired from full-time employment and carried on writing as well as dabbling in examination invigilation in local schools. I have a growing portfolio of books, features, reviews and poetry under my belt, and through the writing I have met and connected with some very impressive people in the media and the arts. I consider myself to have had a reasonably successful working life and a happy life generally, sometimes against the odds.

Many things shape us – formal education, family, sage wisdom from old relatives, religion, news, gossip and all sorts of other ballyhoo. Without a father as mentor and guide, I learned by experience. My mainly retail management career taught me many things: to be reasonably well organised and efficient; to be a reasonably articulate speaker; to listen actively; to think on my feet; to appreciate success and to bounce back from failure. I suppose the times when having a father around might have been useful and comforting were the three occasions I lost jobs. Being able to pick up the phone and talk might have helped me to unravel the disappointment and worry of those times. I have a feeling my father wouldn't have been that great a listener or adviser, but paternal words of wisdom in difficult situations would have been nice. I can say this because I am the father of two sons, David and Steven, who have sought my advice and counsel on various matters over the years. I have been, and always will be, there for them. It works the other way too – I often ask them for their perspective on things.

So in the absence of my father, what other factors influenced and shaped my life? It's time to look way back and connect some ancestral dots.

CHAPTER 5: Belfast

Background

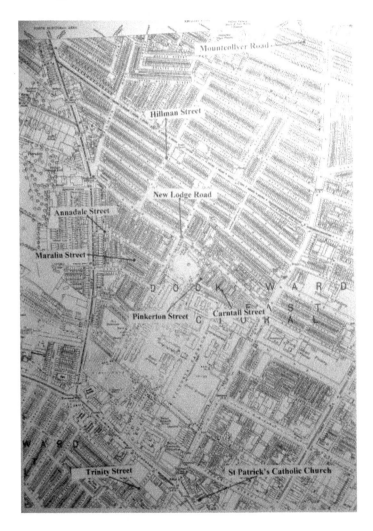

I think it is important to paint in some background to my family's history to convey a sense of people and places. An Ordnance Survey map of Belfast in the 1920s, and an old tourist booklet gives us a sense of place, while the 1911 Census, the latest available for public access online, and birth, marriage and death certificates shed valuable light on and add shape to otherwise shadowy ancestors.

Belfast, the Official Guide, published in 1928, puts a positive spin on Belfast as it tried to progress after the First World War and gives a flavour of the city in the early years of my parents' lives. 'Not only is Belfast exceedingly interesting on account of its docks, fine public buildings, extensive parks and striking industrial developments,' it says, 'but it is also a great centre for sports and an admirable base from which to make excursions by rail and road … the district has the charm of diversified scenery – lake, river, sea coast, hill, valley and mountain – to contribute to his store of happy memories.' Who was to know that economic depression was just around the corner and another terrible world war was just a decade away?

In fact, Belfast of the 1920s was afflicted with ongoing sectarian tension, trouble on the streets, assassinations, violent flare-ups and civil unrest. My great-grandparents, grandparents and parents lived in a very unsettled, sometimes dangerous, city.

The 1920s Ordnance Survey Map of the Dock Ward electoral district of North Belfast shows the density of streets and rows of terrace houses squeezed into what seems like every available space. It was a mainly Catholic area; Mountcollyer, situated to the east and closer to the shipyards, was predominately Protestant. St Patrick's Church on Donegall Street was the venue for most of the official religious services – baptisms, marriages and funerals – in my family's distant past. The church was completed in 1815; at its consecration, the parish priest, Father William Crolly, allegedly told those gathered that £1,300 of the £4,100 cost had been donated by Protestants. Now there's a thing! I visited the church in 2017 to have a look around. Many years have passed since I was there and I wanted to sit on a pew and think of my parents on their happy wedding day. It is a beautiful church and it has the magical ability to increase the volume of Protestant, Orangemen's drums every 12 July! They bang the big drums harder to make an anti-Catholic point.

Most of the two-storey houses in the area would have had the same layout – tiny hallway, small living room, compact kitchen at ground level and two bedrooms and a bathroom up some very steep stairs. Many New Lodge residents worked at the nearby York Street weaving factory or at Gallagher's tobacco factory. The area also featured a huge military base called Victoria Barracks and a poor house (now Clifton House) established by the Belfast Charitable Institution. Some main roads were also tramways.

I knew this area quite well when I was a kid. Around nine or ten years old, I would often travel alone to call in on my relatives. From home in Andersonstown, I would go to the terminus close by and get on a bus to the centre of Belfast. I would get off at Castle Street, walk along Royal Avenue, take a left up North Street, and head for North Queen Street to get to the New Lodge Road. It was quite a distance, but I was young, fit and didn't mind at all. Besides, there were treats to be had. Once I had called in to my granny's and Aunt Sally's, I would head up the New Lodge, turn left into Lepper Street, cross into to Annadale Street, and go down Ashton Street to Maralin Street to see Aunt Bridget. If I started out at one in the afternoon, I would be home by five. It felt like an adventure to me.

Rachel, my mother's mother – my grandmother – lived at 14 Pinkerton Street. The 1911 Census reveals that her father was William Kelly, 48 at the time, and her mother was Mary Ellen, 43. They had four sons: William John, 18; Peter Toal, 15; Anthony, 6; James, 2; and four daughters: Rachel, 14 (my granny); Mary Ellen, 13; Sarah, 8; Margaret, 5. They are all listed as Roman Catholic. (Kelly. A name that features prominently in my mother's ancestry and the chosen 'undercover' surname adopted by my father!)

My great-grandfather was a general labourer and my great-grandmother is listed as a housewife. William John and Peter Toal were shipyard labourers, Rachel and young Mary Ellen were doffers in linen mills. (A doffer was a textile worker who removed full bobbins or cones from textile machines and put in empty ones.) Sarah, Anthony and Margaret were schoolchildren. Everyone could read and write, except Anthony, Margaret and, of course, James.

Apart from Rachel, my granny, the only names familiar to me are Sarah who became known as Aunt Sally, Anthony who became Uncle Tony and Margaret who became Aunt Peg.

Tony was a merchant seaman, which to a youngster like me sounded very romantic as he travelled to that place called 'abroad'. When he came back to Belfast, he would sit in an armchair in my granny's and drink tea. In fact, he was a chain tea-drinker; anytime his cup emptied, someone would scoop it up, head to the scullery and bring back a refill. I seem to remember he was a quiet man. He probably had many stories in his head but he never told them. I imagined adventurous Treasure Island-type excitement, but the truth was probably days of hard work shifting goods from commercial ships to shore and vice versa. He seemed happy enough.

Once they married, Granny Rachel and her sister Sarah lived side by side in houses on the New Lodge Road, numbers 46 and 48 respectively. In 1965, when most of the houses on the street were cited for demolition, they moved further up the New Lodge into the same 13-storey tower block, Alamein House, and lived opposite each other on the same floor.[15]

My mother's father, Thomas (Tommy) Millar, lived at 111 Mountcollyer Road. The 1911 Census states his father was Samuel Millar, 47, and his mother was Martha, 47. They had four daughters: Agnes, 20; Martha, 19; Mary Jane, 11; Lilly, 7; and four sons: Samuel, 15; Hugh, 14; Thomas (my grandfather), 12; William, 9. They are all listed as Methodist (i.e. Protestant).

My great-grandfather, Samuel senior, was a flax spinning overlooker, also known as a spinning master, and Martha was a housewife, Agnes, Samuel and Hugh were mill flax spinners and young Martha was a mill flax threader. Thomas, Mary Jane, William and Lilly were school children. Most of them could read and write. Martha, my great-grandmother, could read only, and the two youngest children were listed as 'cannot read'.

However it happened, Tommy Millar, Methodist, started courting Rachel Kelly, Catholic. Religious conflict was just as rife in Belfast in the early 1900s as it was to become later in the century, and 'mixed' relationships were not only frowned upon, they were actively discouraged with threats and violence. Tommy was subjected to such threats and

---

[15] The name of the tower block, Alamein, was seen by local Republicans as a British military connection too far and, in 1996, with Housing Executive approval, the name was changed to Eithne House, a nod away from British imperialism and towards Irish mythology. Along with flags, marches, and bonfires, these things have always been important issues in certain quarters in Northern Ireland.

found himself on the run to avoid being caught by people, including members of his own family, who intended to do him harm. When he announced that he was going to convert to Catholicism in order to marry Rachel, he really was in deep trouble. He was wary of the routes he took to work and was always watching his back, a burden for anyone, but more so for someone like him, a small man (a tad over five feet), gentle in nature and afflicted with a severe stammer.[16] He dared to fall in love with a girl from 'the other side' and they both survived.

Eventually the threats subsided and Tommy and Rachel married on 17 February 1920 in St Patrick's Church. At the time, Tommy was an oiler, presumably of textile machinery, and Rachel was a spinner. They lived on the New Lodge Road and my mother was born on 7 October 1925. The family comprised an older brother William (Billy), who I never knew, and a younger sister Sheila. Aunt Sheila, who has helped me with several memories for this book, was always close to my mother. At the time of writing, she is still with us, thank goodness, living in a comfortable flat in the same area where she was brought up. Tommy and Rachel were happily married for over fifty years. Tommy died aged 73 in 1972 and Rachel (77) in 1975.

My father's family history is a little more complicated. My great-grandfather John Cushnan married Maggie Saunderson on 8 November 1900. He was 24 and she was 22. He was a pork cutter living at 5 Trinity Street and she was a machinist living at 49 Hartley Street. According to the 1911 Census, the Cushnans lived at 29 Annadale Street, not far from New Lodge Road and by that time they had

---

[16] The stammer was not in evidence at family get-togethers when he sang his party piece 'Nellie Dean', pitch perfect and beautiful.

three daughters: Sarah, 9; Mary, 7; Rosena, 1; and one son, John, 4 (my grandfather). They are listed as members of the Catholic Church. John senior had become a butcher and Maggie was a housewife. Sarah and Mary were schoolchildren. John senior, Maggie and Sarah could read and write. The others were listed as 'cannot read'. On 7th September 1918, Maggie died at the age of 39 at the Royal Victoria Hospital from intestinal obstruction and heart failure.

Meanwhile, on 2 November 1904, Alexander Shannon married Ellen O'Malley. He was 22 and a labourer living at 62 Hillman Street; she was a factory girl living at 2 Carntall Street. The Shannons had three daughters: Bridget, 6; Catherine, 4; Mary, 2. But on 12 February 1911, Alexander Shannon died from 'pulmonary tuberculosis and exhaustion'. Ten years later, on 8 September 1921, his widow Ellen married John Cushnan, widower.

The marriage certificate describes John as a labourer living at 59 Annadale Street and Ellen as a spinner living at 32 Maralin Street. They set up home together at the Annadale Street address. My father was born on 11 February 1925. The three Shannon daughters now had a half-brother.

I have no recollection of Mary, but at some point Bridget and Catherine (Cassie) moved into 20 Maralin Street, a house we grew to know well as kids. Cassie was cranky and a bit sharp with her tongue; I have an image of her always dressed in black. But Aunt Bridget was softly spoken, generous and lovely, and always seemed to be wearing a colourful apron. We visited Bridget once a week and to me her house always smelled of biscuits and marmalade. She would give us half a crown to share. Her catchphrase, when we said something cute or funny was 'Bless the darling' – at least that's my recollection; the rest of my family is convinced that the catchphrase was 'Blessed Ireland'. When my father left us, he spent some time living with Bridget. I have a distant memory of seeing my father in her house. Aunt Bridget took me upstairs where he was ill in bed. I think I kept my distance. I can't be clear about when this happened but it was soon after he left us in 1960. I think she was very upset about my father's behaviour but she was torn between her half-brother and his seven young kids. Aunt Bridget died in 1984; my father died less than two years earlier. I'm not sure she was aware of his passing. It is not out of the question that he kept in touch with her during the 'missing' years but, alas, it is one of many things I will never know.

I don't remember my grandfather John, but a cousin who knew him better described him as a 'Sharp's toffee man' referring to the dapper, bowler-hatted cartoon character used to sell confectionery. By all accounts, my grandfather was a neat dresser out of his working clothes.

So, in the late 1920s and 1930s, my mother and father were growing up, going to school and living during rough times. Belfast was an edgy place, the world was experiencing the effects of the Great Depression and trouble was brewing in Europe. But young kids wouldn't have understood a lot of what was going on locally, nationally and internationally. As long as there was enough to eat and enough time to play outside, life probably felt good.

My parents became teenagers in 1938. That period was known to some as the 'hungry thirties' – jobs were hard to come by and money was tight, especially for working-class families. Living conditions were poor and a substantial number of houses were affected by damp and decay. Some houses were overcrowded, adults and children often sharing bedrooms. Basic amenities were lacking, including hot water and indoor toilets. I recall my granny's house on the New Lodge Road had an outside toilet, a frightening place to have a wee because of the possibility of rats scurrying around. That house also had a tiny scullery, more like what we would now call a utility room and next to the scullery was a large room where the family spent most of its time. There was a dining table at one end and a settee and armchairs at the other. Off to one side was a massive range for cooking, boiling water and washing clothes. The range was on the go all day and kept the house warm. Up towards the ceiling was a clothes drying rack that was lowered and raised by string-pulls. The room at the front of the house was known as the parlour. As kids, we were never allowed in that room. It was the place where ornaments were kept in glass cabinets. It was immaculate, and was only used for important occasions like funeral wakes or a visit from a priest. The staircase up to the bedrooms was narrow but I don't recall much about the bedrooms themselves.

Thinking about the narrow staircase puts me in mind of the house next door, occupied by my granny's sister Sarah Killen, Aunt Sally, and her family. I remember hearing that when my Uncle John Killen died, they had to remove the entire bannister in order to manoeuvre his coffin down the stairs.

My abiding memory of my granny's and my Aunt Sally's houses on the New Lodge Road is of comfort and joy. Both houses were warm and cosy; they were wonderful places to visit. The smells of cooking and stewing tea were always in the air. Aunt Sally's signature dish, as we would say these days, was boiled peas with salt and vinegar, thick slices of bread and butter and a huge mug of dark brown tea. Delicious! Over the years, I have tried to replicate the taste of those peas but I fail every time. Aunt Sheila was responsible for introducing me to exotic food. She would sprinkle curry powder onto bowls of stew. It was outrageous at the time but a great success. Our visits to Aunt Sally's were almost always on Saturday afternoons when wrestling was on TV. She was a great 'grapple' fan and enjoyed the baddies like Mick McManus, Jackie Pallo and Giant Haystacks. She was always running around serving food and clearing up but she would often stop in her tracks to shout at the television when she spotted a dirty move.

As a child I took no particular interest in the condition of the houses. They looked great to me, except the yard where the outside toilets were located. I loved both of them, numbers 46 and 48. People took care of their houses as best they could, especially the step and pavement around the front door. Tiled front steps were cleaned and polished frequently using, if I remember correctly, a red brand of wax polish called Mansion. It was many a housewife's routine to don a pinafore and maybe a head scarf and get to work. It was as much a pride thing as it was good housekeeping. A dirty doorstep suggested the occupants were on the skids or just plain lazy. In addition, the net curtains in the front room window always had to be clean and white.

My sisters, Mary and Geraldine, reminded me of a few other memories from our early days. Directly across the road from numbers 46 and 48 was Mary Ellen's shop, an old-fashioned convenience store that sold groceries, sweets and household goods. I recall being sent over there a few times by Granny Rachel to buy her tins of snuff and to collect free muslin cloths that had covered sides of bacon. Granny would clean the muslin by boiling it furiously on the big range in the back living room, then dry it on the hoisted line and finally cut the cloth into hankies. She had a pretty loud sneeze and enjoyed nothing better than a good nose blow after a snort of snuff. My sisters also remember a Mrs Foy who sold penny and halfpenny glasses of lemonade from her house. A few extra coppers in the tin were always welcome.

In a wider context, the city, as with the rest of Northern Ireland, was dominated by the Unionist Party. Sectarianism was rife, and rioting erupted for all kinds of reasons. In 1935, for example, after a period of increasing tension between Protestants and Catholics, riots disrupted the Twelfth of July Orange parades. In the ensuing days, more than 2,000 people, mainly Catholics, were threatened and had to leave their homes. Many Catholics were forced out of their jobs, and around a dozen people, both Protestant and Catholic, were killed. It must have been a truly frightening time in my parents' lives.

Newspaper photographs of the time show groups of children sitting beside piles of rocks, ready to throw them at a moment's notice; police officers have their pistols drawn ready to shoot; armoured vehicles stand by to transport captured rioters to police stations. Belfast was then, and is still, no stranger to street violence. Bizarrely, only a few years earlier, Protestants and Catholics had joined together to protest against poverty in the Relief Riots. In October 1932, thousands of Protestant and Catholic workers went on strike, showing unity by congregating en masse outside the City Hall to listen to a variety of speakers supporting demands for a living wage and for welfare support (there was no welfare state or national health service). The core message was one of no surrender to poverty, misery and destitution.

Away from trouble, kids had to make their own fun and improvise by being creative with any old junk they found in the streets. There was always a ball to kick about and, in the absence of an actual ball, one could easily be formed out of old rags or scrunched up paper. Among boys, guiders were popular. These rickety transport contraptions comprised a few lengths of wood, some discarded pram wheels and a bit of rope, all connected to each other by a wing and a prayer and guaranteed to be highly dodgy on rough paths or speeding down hills. There wasn't a crash helmet or knee pad in sight.

For some, including my mother and father, bicycles were all the rage; no one thought twice about going off on long jaunts to the coast or out into the countryside. A group of friends, girls and boys, would equip themselves with parcels of sandwiches, bottles of lemonade and hit the open road on a weekend day.

Strict parental controls stated how long teenagers could stay out at a dance or with their friends on street corners. But teenagers being teenagers, they soon worked out how to dupe their parents and found ways to break the rules, even if it meant a hefty smack when they got home. Smoking was cool for boys, and a teenager could strut his stuff to try to attract a girl by puffing away stylishly on a cigarette. Movie stars puffing away on cinema screens just added to the attraction. If it was good enough for Cary Grant, Humphrey Bogart and Clark Gable, it was good enough for young lads. My father was a smoker and he probably picked up the habit when he was in his teens.

Girls, on the other hand, received daily warnings from their mothers about boys and their behaviour. The last thing any family needed in tough financial times was an unmarried pregnant daughter. Alcohol among teenagers did not seem to be the problem it is today. Boozing coincided with young men getting their first jobs. A sort of unwritten tradition emerged that after work, particularly on a Friday, men of all ages would head straight to pubs. Wages were paid in cash and the temptation for porter and wee chasers was too great for the majority. In a way, young rookies were taught how to drink by older soaks.

A number of Catholics, more female that male, chose to become members of the Pioneer Association, an organisation that advocated total abstinence from alcohol, but it's a fair guess that the drinkers, mainly men, outnumbered the abstainers. My mother was a Pioneer all her life. I can't help but think that if my father had been one too, it might have saved their marriage.

In the 1930s, teenagers like my parents had limited choices for entertainment. At home, there may have been a radio and a gramophone. Outside, if there were any spare pennies, concerts, dances and the cinema were entertaining treats. Free leisure activities like walking and cycling were popular pastimes. It may have been a period of great uncertainty both in Northern Ireland and across Europe, but they were happy times for my mother and father.

CHAPTER 6: Margaret Mary 'Rita' Cushnan

My mother in 1980

My mother was born Margaret Mary Millar (but known all her life as Rita) in 1925. She was educated at St Malachy's Primary School on the New Lodge Road, within easy walking distance from home. In her teens, after leaving school, she attended night classes with her Aunt Peg at the 'Black Man Tech' in College Square East, the building taking its nickname from the dark colour of the nearby statue of notable Belfast cleric, Dr Henry Cooke. My mother and Peg were taught sewing and stitching, skills that secured them employment in the local textile factories and that served her well as a housewife and mother.

The bulk of my mother's working life as a full-time employee was during the war years. She was about fifteen when she started in 1940. She worked in the laundry, alongside Aunt Peg, at Langford Lodge US military base about fifteen miles from Belfast and close to Aldergrove Airport, now Belfast International. During the Second World War, Langford was an air depot for the US Air Force, a stopping-off point for planes on their way from America to Africa, the Mediterranean and Europe. At its busiest, in 1943, the base employed around 7,000 military personnel and a substantial number of local civilians, the latter mainly involved in housekeeping and catering activities. I'm sure young Rita was attracted to the handsome Americans with their swagger and twangy accents.

She moved closer to home when she got a job at a company called Beltex, a textile mill in the appropriately named Flax Street in the Ardoyne area that produced ladies' underwear for Etam shops. This mill, like many others, looked like a prison from the outside. Inside, the work was hard and sweaty and the environment was dangerous and noisy. Belfast was famous the world over for linen products, anything from bedding to tea towels. A study by the Women's Resource & Development Agency sheds much light on the textile industry in Belfast, dubbed Linenopolis, in the early twentieth century:

> In the year 1900 there were 900,000
> spindles running in Belfast alone,
> more than in any country in the
> world. There were 35,000 power
> looms in Ulster [compared to]
> 22,000 in Great Britain and the

Continent of Europe combined.
Fifty to sixty thousand women and
girls were employed in linen
production.

Working conditions were appalling and wages were low,
with women earning much less than men (my mother
earned about ten shillings a week). Hours were long and
poor health was a major issue because of the heat and dust.
There was very little patience with pregnant employees,
who were expected to give birth and return to work without
unnecessary delay. The emergence of trade unions and
ensuing campaigns and strikes slowly helped to bring
improvements to pay and working conditions. By the time
my mother started working, not long after the start of the
war, there was increased demand for linen, and that
provided an opportunity for organised workers to campaign
even harder for better pay and conditions. One strike lasted
seven weeks.

However hard the work was, it was a job and there was
much pressure on working-class families to earn wages.
The only alternative was abject poverty. One Friday, my
mother, along with many others, was paid off in a cost-
cutting exercise by Beltex but she was too scared to tell her
mother until the Monday. Luckily, she managed to find
another job on the Monday at the Mayfair factory in Athol
Street, Belfast, just behind Jury's Inn Hotel today. Among
other things, the Mayfair produced St Michael branded
clothes for Marks and Spencer.

It was a time of fear and austerity with a ration book
system controlling what people could buy, particularly with
regard to food. From January 1940, rationing affected the
purchase of many basics – butter, sugar, meat, fish, dairy,

tea, breakfast cereals, flour, jam and fruit. Sweets and chocolate were soon added to the list. In an attempt to make up the shortfall, the public was encouraged to Dig for Victory – to dig up their front and back gardens and turn them over to growing vegetables. Schools and universities joined this campaign too and soon, cabbages, carrots and potatoes appeared where once there had been green lawns. Pigs, chickens, rabbits and even goats were reared in gardens in towns and cities. Ironically, the war-time diet, while monotonous, has since been deemed one of the healthiest ever. With unhealthy fat and sugar in short supply and only wholesome ingredients available, people were forced to eat healthier meals. The New Lodge Road, Annadale Street and Maralin Street houses did not have front and back gardens, so they had to rely on neighbours and friends to supplement their store cupboards. In desperate times, there was also the black market. My parents grew up in very tough times in a sometimes tough neighbourhood and they survived it all – even the Belfast Blitz in 1941.

But it was not all doom and gloom. My mother loved going out to dances, especially ceilis at the Ard Scoil in Divis Street. This was a Catholic boys club that ran regular events. Wooden floorboards and hard-heeled Irish dancing shoes made them noisy affairs, not to mention the rousing music accompanied by yos and yelps as dancers swung each other around the room. It was a time for boys and girls to meet under close supervision.

One story goes that my mother went to St Mary's on the Hill, Glengormley, with her friends, and after the dance they all decided to walk home (perhaps to save a few pennies), claiming they had missed the last tram. The distance was roughly six miles down the Antrim Road. My mother told Granny Rachel the fib and went to bed.

According to Aunt Sheila, my mother talked about it in her sleep and let the cat out of the bag. Sharp-eared Granny overheard and 'nearly killed her'.

In the 1940s, my mother, the teenager, was an avid cinemagoer. She frequented the Capital, on the Antrim Road, the Lyceum on the New Lodge Road and the Duncairn in Duncairn Gardens where a few pennies got you in. The films she might have seen included *Snow White and the Seven Dwarfs*, Errol Flynn in *The Adventures of Robin Hood*, James Cagney in *Angels with Dirty Faces*, Robert Donat in *Goodbye, Mr Chips* and the epic *Gone With The Wind* starring Clark Gable. She once told me that her favourite film star was John Payne.

My best estimate of when my parents met and started courting is when they were in their mid-teens and socialising at dances, church youth activities and visits to the pictures. That would be in 1943 or so, maybe a bit later. It is impossible to pinpoint the timing exactly but a rough estimate is the best I can come up with. I would guess they hung around regularly with a group of friends and romances developed gradually. But, eventually, they were married on 16 September, 1947 at St. Patrick's Church. I will return to the wedding later but mention that from 1947, they had thirteen years together in the same home. Even after my father walked out in 1960, the marriage stayed intact legally. Divorce was never an option.

My mother was raised and schooled as a Catholic and quite religious. But she became even more religious after my father left. In addition to Sunday mass, she would visit the church throughout the week and hold regular family rosary sessions in the evenings. Her faith and prayers gave her hope and comfort, hope that even when times were tough help was at hand, and comfort that in the dark moments

God was watching over us. Without her faith, my mother may well have struggled to cope, especially when we were young, needy and demanding. Our local church, St. Teresa's, was pretty much a hop, skip and a jump from our front door over the Glen Road. It is one of the great symbols of my childhood. The dominant figure there in my memory was Canon Gerard McNamara, a formidable chap who had what they now call 'presence'.

My mother had part-time jobs to supplement the family income. At one time she cleaned a couple of nearby houses; she was also a dinner lady at St Teresa's Primary School close by. I remember her as a very active, busy lady. She had no choice, I suppose. She was not a driver, but she could fair canter down the Glen Road to the shops and back. Her soup and stew recipes were legendary in our family circle and her baking – apple tarts, rhubarb tarts and currant (curn) squares – were amazing. She knitted at every possible moment; the click of needles often accompanied whatever was on the radio or, later, the television. Aran jumpers were her forte. During breaks from knit-one-purl-one, she would stuff the knitting and needles down the side of the settee. One time, I jumped on the settee and was immediately stabbed in the back of the leg. There was blood, but my mother stuck a plaster over the wound, wiped the bloodied needle and carried on knitting. When I was twelve, I was obsessed with the American TV group The Monkees. Their television show was a crazy mix of comedy and music, and it was very successful. My favourite Monkee was Mike Nesmith who always wore a dark green bobble hat. I wanted one just like it. My mother took up the challenge and produced an exact replica. When she handed it to me, you should have seen my face. I was a believer! (I couldn't resist that.) I was chuffed and wore it as much as I could, which, let me tell you, required a lot of courage on the streets of Andersonstown, Belfast.

During stressful periods of her life, she took up smoking, often nipping to the bathroom to blow the smoke out of the window. At family parties, I remember her singing 'The Green Glens of Antrim' and 'Forty Shades of Green'.

At times after my father left in 1960 she was strapped for cash. One day she handed me a folded piece of paper and told me to take it down the street to a neighbour. I would have been around seven or eight. Along the way I opened the paper and read the scribbled note. She was asking the neighbour to lend her some money. I folded the paper, carried on walking and delivered it to its intended recipient. It meant nothing to me. I had no understanding of money or debt or hardship. But now, looking back on the memory, it makes me shiver to think that she had been reduced to asking for money.

Every Tuesday afternoon, I think it was, a big noisy lorry would pull up outside the house and a few minutes later, the latch would go on our shed door in the yard, followed by the sound of a mini-avalanche as Sammy the coal man tipped a delivery into the bay. Then he would knock the back door for his money. I remember his face covered in black coal dust and a wide yellow-toothed smile as he chatted with my mother for a few minutes.

Winter was also the season of the paraffin smell. It was when the old heater was dusted down and I got to enjoy – under mother's supervision – the danger of putting a match to the wick and lighting the blue flame. The hall was draughty and the heater was essential.

My mother loved bingo. It was a night out locally with her friends and a chance to win some money. She did win occasionally – nothing huge like the jackpot, but more modest (and very welcome) sums in the region of twenty pounds. When she got home, you could tell by her smile that she was chuffed.

She was not overtly political and had little time for rabble-rousing. She had no time at all for the Reverend Ian Paisley, the Free Presbyterian Church firebrand who shouted and bawled his way through his political career, until he evolved into a much calmer elder statesman. In the late 60s and the 1970s, he was a very threatening sight and sound to many Catholics. My mother, otherwise incapable of hatred, recoiled when Paisley came on the local television news. One day, he was shouting his mouth off about something or other and my mother, exasperated, took off one of her slippers and flung it at the TV, hitting the Reverend square in the face. We kids gaped at her in shock and amazement. It must have been very satisfying, if uncharacteristic, moment for her.

When I left school at sixteen and got my first job, my mother would be up very early to make sure I got my breakfast and caught the bus on time. She carried on doing this for several years even though I was perfectly capable of looking after myself. But that was her way.

At family gatherings in the 1960s and 1970s, it was almost compulsory for everybody attending to do a party piece. The routine would be for the singer to sing the first line or two and then everybody in the room joined in. There were always guitars around, played mostly by my cousins Bill, John and David Tierney, who would lead us in a mixture of Irish rebel songs, country and folk numbers and a few popular tunes of the day. My mother would sing too, 'The Green Glens of Antrim' and 'Forty Shades of Green', and as I recall she had a slight but lovely singing voice and was pitch-perfect.

She was a creature of habit when it came to her choice of daily newspaper. In Belfast, there were two morning papers, the *News Letter*, a Unionist/Protestant favourite, and *The Irish News*, the preference of Nationalists/Catholics. So *The Irish News* it was and, in common with just about everybody who read it, it was straight to the obituaries page to check out any familiar names. The old joke was that if your own name was not in the list, you could get on with your day. Her other regular reading material included the *People's Friend* for the good short stories, *The Weekly News* for a variety of features and *The Sunday Post*, Scotland's Sunday newspaper that included the favourite cartoon strips Oor Wullie and The Broons. She felt some affinity with the Scots for reasons that are hard to define as we didn't have any Scottish connections that I knew of. She enjoyed the music, the shortbread and Edinburgh rock confectionery. She would never miss *The White Heather Club* song and dance show on television presented by Andy Stewart, and New Year celebrations weren't quite complete without an appearance by Stewart singing 'Come in, come in, it's nice to see you. How's yourself, you're looking grand.'

Books were not a big thing in our home until much later. My mother allowed us loads of comics – *Bunty* for the girls (although I liked that one too), *Valiant* for the boys with its action stories, and *Beano*, *Dandy* and *Beezer* for all of us. Mary Wilson in the upstairs flat would share other magazines with my mother like *Red Letter* and *Red Star*, both romantic fiction magazines. Mary also used to give us bags of Vienna fruit bonbons, American sweets I think – hard candy on the outside with a soft goo on the inside. They seemed quite posh compared to the more common sweets like butter balls, clove rock and midget gems.

In her eighties, Rita fell victim to dementia and was cared for by my three wonderful sisters, Mary, Geraldine and Sheila, who devoted all of their time to her. At least one of them was with her every minute of every day. It was exhausting but done with love and loyalty and without complaint. As one of my sister's put it: 'She looked after us all those years and now it's our turn to do the same for her.'

My mother died, aged 86, on 29 December 2011, my three sisters with her until the end. When the coffin left the Bingnian Drive flat, her home for six decades, the street outside was packed with people waiting to pay their respects. It was very moving. St Teresa's was bunged to the rafters. She was well known, well liked, popular and pretty much a fixture in that part of Andersonstown. The service was beautiful and sincere. Afterwards, she was cremated at Roselawn Crematorium, about eight miles away and her ashes buried in the same Milltown grave as her own mother and father.

In my mind, though, she continues to be a point of reference if I need to think something through or make an important decision. In the absence of a father, my mother must take most of the credit for the kind of boy I was and the kind of man I became.

In a recent radio interview, when I'd been invited to talk about my missing father, I was asked: 'Did your mother not consider remarrying?'

The short answer is no. It would never have occurred to her because of her Catholicism. The Catholic Church does not permit divorce for sacramental marriages, unions that are decreed impossible to dissolve. (The teaching is that two become one flesh joined by God, and no human has the power or authority to separate them.) In a difficult relationship, living apart is acceptable but that's about it.

Despite its complications, my mother held to that belief throughout her life. I suspect my father considered he was as good as divorced when he walked out. It is not clear if his Catholicism lapsed, but my mother's faith never wavered.

My mother never mentioned my father, and I have no idea what she thought of him. That is an interesting point in itself. She would happily tell stories about the old days but he was erased in the telling.

Many times while writing this book I have found myself wishing that previous generations of my family had written more down, had kept diaries or secret journals. But alas, they didn't and so their versions of events were buried with them. But we do have photographs.

CHAPTER 7: Photograph Album

Note: All of the photographs in this chapter are photographs of old photographs. The quality is not great, but I chose to include them anyway.

My wife and I have been sorting out loft and drawer clutter, but it has taken a lot longer to do than we imagined because whenever we unearthed boxes of photographs we just had to stop and pore over them. There are hundreds of shots from our courting days and our married life, and photos of our sons at various stages of their young lives. There are lots of holiday snaps, the camera we used thoughtfully imprinting on them a date stamp. If anyone wanted to research my life story, the material in these boxes would be a godsend. In contrast, research for this book about my father has been hugely challenging; even precise details of my mother's early life are elusive.

But there are photographs, which, with a little detective work, can help flesh out the story. If life is like a movie, photographs freeze moments in time that, assembled in some kind of rough chronological order, become a showcase of lives lived.

There are a few photographs of my mother and father, both separately and together. These photographs were found by my brother Kevin in 2017, some seventy years after they were taken. I had always imagined my father as a dour man, a moody, tense individual. But these images, in which he is smiling so genuinely, have forced me to reassess my preconceptions. The sepia-tinted photos that follow were probably taken in the mid-1940s, before they married in 1947.

Both my mother and father and their circle of friends liked cycling and it was not uncommon for them at weekends to journey miles out of Belfast into the country or to a beach on the coast. The bicycles would not have been expensive or especially comfortable. To spend hours on them and travel miles would have been a major feat of endurance in the name of leisure. Aunt Sheila, my mother's sister, recalled jaunts to places like Carnlough, 34 miles away from Belfast, and Cushendall, 47 miles away. This photograph shows my father, relaxed and happy, leaning on the handlebars of his bike.

Here he is again, smiling away alongside my mother. His bicycle clips suggest this was taken on a cycling trip and it shows my parents were very happy together at that time. I love my mother's sensible shoes. I like this photograph especially because it captures my mother and father, then boyfriend and girlfriend, larking about. It's such a wonderful moment.

This shot is a joy to look at. My father dominates the picture, cigarette in hand, surrounded by girls. My mother is on the right, clearly happy among friends (I don't know who the others are.)

Here's my mother with friends on a beach, maybe at Cushendall. I love the movie-star pose, the sunglasses and her obvious happiness. I like to imagine someone, perhaps my father, calling her name and catching her by surprise.

Here's another lovely snap with my mother in the middle with two friends who might have been factory workmates. It looks as though they're standing outside a pub. My mother was always smiling!

The only photo that can be dated exactly is the one taken on my parents' wedding day, Tuesday 16 September 1947. The wedding registration certificate records that John Cushnan, 22, bachelor, of 20 Maralin Street, married Margaret Mary Millar, 22, spinster, of 46 New Lodge Road. The priest conducting the service was Father Richard O'Neill.

The wedding photo has obviously been staged by a professional photographer. On the far left is best man Gerry Savage. Next to him is Marie (pronounced Marry) Killen, my mother's cousin (although we kids always referred to her as our cousin). My father is standing, his hand on back of my mother's chair, and on the far right is 'Aunt' Sheila Millar, my mother's sister. My father is on the verge of a smile, my mother and her sister both look very happy and beautiful. The wedding ceremony took place at St. Patrick's Catholic Church, Donegall Street, Belfast, at nine o'clock in the morning. According to *The Irish News* that day, it was cool with scattered showers and a bit of a breeze.

111

After the service, there was a brief breakfast reception, followed by a one-night honeymoon in Dublin. I don't know much about my father's friendship with Gerry Savage, his best man. Gerry married Mary McCusker and they later moved to America, where Gerry worked for Chevrolet in Michigan and Mary in the garment industry.

After my parents' wedding in 1947 they lived with Granny Rachel and Granda Tommy at 46 New Lodge Road, along with Aunt Sheila and Uncle Billy. That was quite a tight squeeze for a terraced house with three modest-sized bedrooms. In time, things got even tighter. Paul was born in 1949. I think my father is holding my brother Paul in the image above. Father is wearing a smart suit and Paul is dressed up to the nines, suggesting that this snap was most likely taken on the day of his christening. My father would have been 24.

The following year, my brother Sean arrived, and in 1951 my sister Mary was born, three more inhabitants at No. 46.

It would have been clear by that time that the number of people outweighed the living space and so the hunt began for an alternative Cushnan residence.

The Andersonstown estate, about four miles from Belfast city centre, was just developing at that time and my parents managed to secure a council flat at 170 Bingnian Drive. They moved in on 19 March 1952. It was a ground-floor flat in a block of four near the bus terminus, and only a short walk to St Teresa's church and close to St Teresa's Primary School. Above us lived the Wilsons, across from them lived the Cunninghams, and below them the O'Neills.

The flat had a living room, a kitchen, a bathroom, three bedrooms and a long hall. At the back was a coal shed and a fair patch of garden, with another garden at the front. Our family had little interest in gardening, so both gardens were mainly grass.

My mother had a full-time job on her hands as a housewife while my father continued to work in the textile industry as a cloth cutter. Apparently, he worked for a time in a place on the Donegall Road that made police uniforms. It must have been risky for a Catholic to be employed in such work, but nothing untoward seemed to have happened as a result of it.

Seven months after moving into Bingnian Drive, my sister Geraldine was born. I followed in 1954, my sister Sheila in 1955 and brother Kevin in 1958. John, Rita and a brood of seven made up the Cushnans.

This photograph, taken in 1957 in our Bingnian Drive living room, is a rare thing indeed. It is rare because it is the only shot of our family together, with the exception of my brother Kevin who hadn't been born yet. It's such a shame there isn't a full Cushnan family photo.

From the left: Sean, Geraldine (with the doll), my father, Mary (in front of Father), me, my mother, Sheila (on Mother's knee) and Paul on the far right. The two wing men, Sean and Paul, along with Mary and my mum get top marks in the smiles department. Bang in the middle, sitting on my father's knee, I look rather startled. It's a great photograph and records a happy, relaxed time.

Our place in Bingnian Drive was at the top of the street, very convenient for the shop across the road run by Dessie McErlean, a local businessman who also owned a lucrative bakery. The Popular – or The Pop as the shop was known – sold a variety of groceries, confectionery, fresh bread, magazines and newspapers.

For about eight years, nine of us lived at Bingnian Drive. My parents had their own room, the girls shared another and the boys had what I think was the biggest room at the front. Bunk beds and shared beds were a must to maximise space. The kitchen was small but a hive of industry, with my mother busy cooking and baking the most delicious, mouth-watering food. She could work miracles with a few ingredients.

The living room had a big front window looking out onto the street. We had a coal fire and comfortable furniture. Dotted around on the sideboard, the window sill and small tables were religious artefacts, and from the walls two images dominated. One was the famous and striking Sacred Heart of Jesus picture and the other was a painting of St Martin De Porres. I could never figure out why my mother had chosen Martin from all the available saints. I think it was because she was a big fan of Pope John XXIII who canonised this Peruvian lay brother of the Dominican Order in 1962, not long after my father left her. St Martin could have been the new pin-up boy of hope. It seems that St Martin is the patron saint of mixed races, barbers, innkeepers, public health workers and those seeking racial harmony. Whatever he meant to my mother, he was always on the wall looking over us.

Not long before my father walked out, I recall him coming home one evening worse for wear after a session in the pub. He wanted his dinner. My mother started to cook sausages for him, but they had an argument (I don't know what it was about) and, as he lay on the settee in a stupor, Mum told him she was taking the kids out for some fresh air so he needed to keep an eye on the frying pan. Some time later, we returned home and were greeted by a blanket of foggy smoke when we opened the front door. My father had fallen asleep and the sausages had burned in the pan.

Having cooled down after the argument and the walk, my mother must have blown a gasket.

The main reasons cited for marriage breakdowns include infidelity, money matters, poor communication, constant arguments and abuse. Infidelity wasn't a factor in my parents' case, but the other four played a part to a greater or lesser degree. I have no evidence whatsoever that my father was physically abusive to my mother but he may well have been a threatening presence, especially when he was drunk. I would wager, though, that his appalling behaviour as a husband and father constituted emotional abuse. I shiver to think about how many times my mother was at the end of her tether worrying about us and how she could afford to feed us. Even before he left, she must have felt the burden of being a single parent.

By the end of the 1950s, booze and betting became my father's only hobbies. I couldn't say whether or not my father was an alcoholic, but he was certainly a slave to alcohol. He had a craving for it. He probably thought of a few drinks after a day's work as some kind of reward. Staying in the pub probably seemed better than going home to a noisy bunch of kids and an obviously unhappy wife. What a contrast when you compare the tensions of their last years together with the happy photographs of their courting days.

As the pressures of earning a wage to provide for his family grew, my father's alcohol consumption increased to the point where he was drinking away good money that was needed for rent, household bills, food, and other family necessities. Taking an educated guess, I'd say that most of the rows were about money. Both my father and my mother would have been exasperated, my mother because she couldn't manage the home and the kids without enough money, and my father because he was feckless and hated being nagged.

The drink, the horses, and sheer carelessness built up to such an extent that something had to give in the marriage. Unable to meet his parental responsibilities and inept with money, he took what I can only describe as the coward's way out. I don't know if there was ever any discussion in an attempt to save the marriage. Somehow I doubt it. I'm not even sure if his decision to leave was a planned thing, where he gave notice to my mother, or whether it was a spur of the moment action. I have a vague memory – it's so vague I could well be inventing it – of him standing in the hall in a long fawn overcoat and carrying a brown suitcase. I don't remember him saying goodbye. We probably just went back to our toys; for us, it was no big deal.

Eventually, he made the decision to leave Bingnian Drive. Heaven knows how my mother felt that night and in the days that followed. In 1960, it would have been very embarrassing for a marriage to break up; there would have been a huge sense of shame attached to it. There she was, abandoned by her husband of thirteen years, with seven kids ranging from 10 to 2 and not a lot of money. There was family allowance which paid benefits of around 10 shillings per child, but it wasn't enough. As soon as she could, my mother took on several part-time jobs to supplement her income. She also had to be thrifty and finds way to spend whatever money she had wisely.

She gave everything she had to look after us and she did it heroically and with love.

CHAPTER 8: London Calling

What I do know is that after leaving Bingnian Drive, my father went straight to Aunt Bridget's house in Maralin Street and used that address as his base for possibly up to a year. He continued to work in Belfast and, no doubt, continued to drink and back horses. He might well have given Aunt Bridget a few quid every week, but there would not have been any pressure or nagging from her about money or paternal responsibilities. She would have been a soft touch for him.

Sometime in 1961 or early 1962, he made the decision to move to England. It could be that chatter among workmates gave him the idea to go 'over the water' to get away from any family responsibilities and to earn good money. The order by Lisburn Petty Sessions Court to pay child support may have helped him to make up his mind. Only a cold and calculating man could suddenly decide to abdicate both of his roles.

I am pretty sure he chose to sail rather than fly, purely because of the expense involved. He had options to sail on the *Ulster Prince* or *Ulster Monarch* to Liverpool, or he could have gone to Glasgow or Ardrossan on the *Royal Scotsman* or *Royal Ulsterman*. Larne–Stranraer was also a possibility. My hunch is that he travelled to Liverpool and eventually made his way south to London, doing odd jobs as he went to keep afloat. There was a hint or two that he may have grafted on the merchant ships to pay his way.

He would have been aware that there were Irish communities in London, places like Cricklewood, Kilburn and Clapham, among others. He settled on Clapham. It was better for a man with an Irish accent, even an Ulster Irish one, to find a place to fit in and not stick out like a sore thumb. It was also an opportunity to ditch the unusual Cushnan name in case anyone in authority came looking for him. I have not found any evidence to suggest that he was some sort of a fugitive on the run, nothing as adventurous and romantic as that. He was more a jack-the-lad, 'sod it, I'm off' kind of man. My father became John Kelly from Derry and set about blending in to his new Irish community.[17] He would have been in his late thirties by this stage.

The playwright Jimmy Murphy published a piece in the *Irish Times* in 2016 about his own experiences of moving to London in the 1970s. He recalled seeing 'Paddies' in their forties and fifties in the pubs around Kilburn who were 'lost in a corner, a darker, quieter, older tribe, still fit and strong but aged way beyond their years from hard graft and harder drinking.' They were men who had lost their way, latching on to each other 'as if to stop themselves

---

[17] Kelly is the second most popular Irish surname after Murphy and before O'Sullivan.

sinking into the abyss.' As the work dried up, these veterans found themselves without much income 'too old for building sites and too poor for the bars. They returned to their bedsits and slowly vanished.'[18]

In her book, *An Unconsidered People: The Irish in London* (2003), Catherine Dunne writes that in the 1950s, it's estimated that of the half million people, mostly men, who emigrated to the UK from Ireland, around eighty per cent headed to areas of London such as Kilburn, Cricklewood, Camden, Edgware and Brent north of the Thames, and as the 1960s progressed more went to Lambeth and Clapham Common. There was a kind of mantra – 'we never meant to stay' – but huge numbers found themselves remaining for decades, many until their dying days. That was around the time when those horrible boarding-house signs allegedly appeared: 'No cats. No dogs. No children. No Irish. No blacks'. The agenda was work, accommodation and then social interaction. Irish clubs evolved such as the Galtymore in Cricklewood, the National in Kilburn, the Blarney on Tottenham Court Road, the Innisfree in Ealing, and the Hibernian at Fulham Broadway. If homesickness, loneliness and depression created the pain, alcohol was the anaesthetic, and so pubs became community hubs.

My father's story was not so much one of going to London to earn money to send home; he was escaping and, in the process, erased his Belfast family. And while quite a few 'never meant to stay', my father had no intentions of going back home to his original life.

---

[18] 'Is a play about a group of Irish men lost in Kilburn still relevant?' *Irish Times*, 10 February 2016. < https://www.irishtimes.com/life-and-style/abroad/generation-emigration/is-a-play-about-a-group-of-irish-men-lost-in-kilburn-still-relevant-1.2529399 >.

I recall my own experience of moving from Belfast to Manchester in February 1976. Almost immediately my Belfast accent sounded abnormal. I was indeed that stranger in a strange land with the added pressure of being easily identifiable as a native of a very troubled part of the United Kingdom. In the early months, I was asked if I was 'on the run' or 'a member of the IRA'. Sometimes it was in a half-joking way but occasionally the questioning was very uncomfortable. I felt vulnerable. So what did I do?

I made the decision to 'go native', to practice sounding 'English' and take the rough edges off my Northern Irish accent. It was a cowardly thing to do in some ways, I suppose, but I was conscious that my accent in the mid-1970s in England was more of a liability than an asset. I had to do something, if only for my own confidence. I listened to my voice, practised certain vowel sounds and tried for a more middle-of-the-road accent. I can't help the way I talk now and I don't worry about it anymore. But I know from first-hand experience that people trying to make a new life in another country come up against all sorts of prejudices and it can be a difficult and challenging period of adjustment.

I wanted to get a feel for the Clapham area, where my father lived, I think, from the tail end of the 1960s until he died in 1982. I went to the Lambeth Archives, housed in the Minet Library, to scour microfilm reels of old newspapers and to look at books and other material. I also wanted to grasp events in a wider sense, things that were happening in the world while he was getting on with his runaway life.

In the news during this time was the Cuban missile crisis (1962), the assassination of President Kennedy (1963), England winning the World Cup (1966), the Apollo 11 moon landing (1969), the UK changing to decimal currency

(1971), Bloody Sunday (1972) and many other terrible atrocities in Northern Ireland, Margaret Thatcher becoming Prime Minister (1979), the Brixton riots (1981), and the Falklands War (spring 1982). I imagine my father skimming the pages of the *Daily Mirror* to note some of these happenings on his way to the horse racing pages.

Television was showing programmes like *Grandstand*, *New Faces*, *Sale of the Century*, *Kojak*, and *That's Life!* My father's time in Clapham coincided with that era of famous horses Arkle, Red Rum and Nijinsky. Peter O'Sullevan's commentary of the races probably boomed out of the television set on the Rose and Crown wall. Who knows what my father won and lost at the bookies. There were opportunities to see some of the touring cabaret acts of the time such as Frankie Vaughn, Peters and Lee, Roy Hudd, and Larry Grayson, who all played Clapham at one time or another.

I wanted to remind myself what the cost of living was like around that time and I based my observations on the year 1976 to get some kind of an average for the decade and because it was the year I left Belfast for England to pursue my career. From that year on, my father and I were living on the same soil again.

From job adverts in local newspapers I reckon that my father would have earned £35–£40 per week. The weekly rent for his bedsit would have been around £5, perhaps a little more. In the 1970s, he would have paid £3 for a basic shirt and the same for a jumper. A standard two-piece suit would set him back anything from £20 to £30. Had my father been a car owner, he would have paid 70p for a gallon of petrol and if he had rented a TV, it would have cost him £3 per week.

It is clear from my research that my father's wages were spent mostly on rent, cigarettes, alcohol and betting. If he had been a regular grocery shopper, he may well have used the newly refurbished Tesco store in Northcote Road, Clapham, which opened in 1976. Even basics would not have cost him too much: TyPhoo tea was 9p, a loaf of bread was 14p, a tin of Heinz tomato soup was 11p, and four small cans of lager were 44p. He might even have stretched to a new shirt at £1.99.

While my father made the decision to erase his family background and change his identity to John Kelly, all his official papers – employment, tax and bank details had to be in the name of Cushnan. Within a short time he found employment as a handyman, first with Nestle and later with the Express Lift Company, secured a bedsit in Clapham and started to frequent the local pub where he steadily built up a new circle of friends.

Clapham is in south-west London and was home at one time or another to various famous people such as diarist Samuel Pepys, composer Edvard Grieg, and writers Graham Greene and Angela Carter. When the railways arrived, Clapham became one of a number of areas favoured by London commuters. It gained a reputation as a suburb of so-called average people. 'The man on the Clapham omnibus' became a phrase associated with the definition of an ordinary, law-abiding nondescript person, a kind of standard definition of ordinariness. Clapham Common is the area's main feature, over 200 acres of green space, mature trees, footpaths, ponds and a Victorian bandstand.

From what I have been able to learn, he lived, socialised and, possibly, worshipped within a few streets of Clapham Common.

6 Orlando Road
(last address)

Rose and Crown Pub
2 The Polygon

The Royal British Legion
154 Victoria Rise

St Mary's RC Church
8 Clapham Park Road

In the blue folder I was given after his death, I found receipts for his subscriptions to the Royal British Legion Clapham branch (annual 55p). They show his name as J. Kelly or R. J. Kelly and they confirm his address as 6 Orlando Road, Clapham. The four key locations in his Clapham life are all with a few streets of each other. His stomping ground took in the Royal British Legion, the Rose and Crown pub, St Mary's church and his bedsit. He may or may not have been a regular churchgoer, but a lot of his pub friends were from Irish Catholic origins, so it's not out of the question that if they went to mass, he did too. His funeral service was held at St Mary's.

In December 2016, I walked in my father's footsteps. I found Orlando Road and the large Victorian building, No. 6, that housed half a dozen bedsits in the 1960s and 1970s. The street is leafy, wide and not unattractive. In the local annals it was described as 'a mixture of semi-detached and terraced, two or three storeys or single storey bays, attractive tiled panels between pairs of doors (especially 6–16) balustraded balconies over bays and decorative cornices.' It sounds quite luxurious. But such notions in the 1970s were a little deceiving.

6 Orlando Road, Clapham, 2016

As I was hovering outside No. 6, a woman walked up to the front door and I was able to find out from the owner, when she opened the door to her visitor, that the building was no longer a collection of bedsits but was now one house and had been that way for many years. I didn't want push my luck with the owner of the house by asking to have a look inside. I suspect one or two interior design changes occurred in the past three decades.

I have no information on Clapham house prices or any idea about rent in the 1970s. My father would have opted for the cheapest accommodation he could find, I have little doubt about that, and a bedsit would have been ideal. The whole idea of a bedsit is to sleep in it and not spend any longer than necessary in a small room to avoid stir craziness.

In *Clapham in the Twentieth Century* (2002), members of the Clapham Society recall the area in the 1960s and 1970s. One described a flat (rather than a bedsit) in a similar house in a street not far from Orlando Road, which helps to give some idea of the conditions my father might have lived in:

> We had a front room facing the street, a back room facing the yard, a dining room and a scullery. There was no bathroom. We had our baths in a five-foot tin receptacle which was a relic from pre-war days, I'm sure. We had nothing else so just made do. There was the option for people living in residences without baths to go to public facilities once a week for a good wash. We had an

outside toilet. There was no privacy
and there were many embarrassing
moments.[19]

The rent was around £2 per week. The member describes
the area as 'a genuine community of people living in semi-
poverty.' Another remembers heating rooms with a not
very efficient gas fire in the days before central heating
became the norm. Other contributors talk about the
'community spirit' in the area and recalls how neighbours
knew and looked out for each other. Front doors were left
open, family and friends were welcome to drop in anytime
and there was a general air of trust. There was crime,
mostly petty theft, occasional burglaries and street fracas
after the pubs closed, but, says one member, compared to
crime in 2002, they were better times. Youth clubs, social
clubs, bingo and pubs all played their parts.

My father was a regular – perhaps too regular – at the
Rose and Crown on a street called The Polygon, practically
at the end of Orlando Road. This was the pub that hosted
my father's wake in 1982. I popped in on a Saturday
lunchtime and, although there was a mixture of accents –
English, Australian, Canadian and Irish – every one of the
customers was male. The pub, dating back to 1870, is fairly
small and was dimly lit. I asked the current landlord a few
questions, but he knew nothing about those days and the
few names I reeled off were received with a shoulder shrug.
In nearly forty years, who knows how many landlords have
leaned on the pumps.

---

[19] The Clapham Society, *Clapham in the Twentieth Century* (2002).

The Rose & Crown, Clapham, 2016,

During the time it took me to drink two pints of beer, I tried
to imagine the banter and blether of 1970s' crowd amid a
haze of cigarette and pipe smoke. There would certainly
have been chat about the situation back in Northern Ireland
and all sorts of ideas and suggestions about who to bless
and who to blame – from a safe distance, of course. Self-
appointed comedians would have exchanged one-liners and
there were probably arguments about almost anything.
There would have been pints and cigarettes cadged and a
lot of swearing as betting slips were scrunched up.

The Royal British Legion, Clapham Branch

From Royal British Legion membership cards I found in the blue folder, I learned that he frequented the Clapham branch at 154 Victoria Rise from 1973 until his death in 1982. He was an associate member for no real reason, I suspect, other than the subsidised booze.

The Legion was founded by veterans after the First World War to help service men and women, veterans and their families in almost every aspect of daily life. If my father had had a son who joined the armed forces, then that would have been his ticket to membership. But he had erased his family in Belfast from his life, hadn't he? And in any case, none of us had been in the army forces. At our father's wake, Kevin and I were approached by a man who asked: 'Which one of you is the son in the navy?' It was certainly neither Kevin nor me. Could it be the unidentified boy whose photograph I had found in the blue folder? A son in the services would certainly be an easy ticket to British Legion membership.

*One of the photographs found in the blue folder.
Could this be my half-brother?*

129

The entrance to St Mary's Church, Clapham

I don't know if my father was a practising Catholic, but if he had been a churchgoer, frequent or infrequent, he would have attended St Mary's. It is a beautiful church with a tall spire – a Clapham landmark. God knows – quite literally, I suppose – how many times he walked in and out of the entrance. He was certainly carried out in a coffin in 1982.

The Clapham Society kindly allowed me to advertise in their monthly bulletin that I was looking for people who knew my father or who could provide information about the 1960s and 1970s in the area. Two respondents, in particular, were very helpful for my quest. They have both asked for discretion, so I have named them 'Sue' and 'Peter' here.

Sue was very familiar with the Rose & Crown:

> Many of the Irish men that were customers at the Rose and Crown in the 60s and 70s were complex characters. Most had left Ireland to

make money in London, many on the various building sites, but they usually spent it and had little savings. Some came into the pub every evening as it was warm and friendly, as many lived alone in damp bedsitters. Not surprisingly their physical and mental health deteriorated. I certainly heard of men changing their names and remarrying in the UK. These were bigamous relationships as they had never divorced their Irish wives. I suppose it was expensive to do so, and not possible if you were from the South. If they were caught, they risked prison and any new children would be deemed illegitimate.

So many single Irish men hid their histories and no one asked probing questions. I heard they were surprised to find that your dad had another name but they may not have been shocked. Many Irish fathers who lived in London saw racing, drinking and gambling as their priorities.

My own father was no exception. He would have helped

with your dad's funeral, maybe even paid for it, as he was a friend and loyal to him, but he was not able to show the same commitment to his own family. My parents separated in the mid-1970s.

The pub had only a male landlord and became a predominately male domain as there was no authoritative female to curb the drinking and gambling. There was a TV on in the pub for the horse races on Saturday and the landlord had a hotline to the local bookies so he could take bets from the customers. He and his male friends sometimes went to the races together. I feel sure that your father would have been part of this crowd.

As for women, well they didn't really fit into the picture very much. My own father had a misogynistic view of the world coupled with racism. He also held that religion was women's business. My mother, like many of her generation, was a practising Catholic. Myself and my three brothers are all atheists. This was the only way we followed our father's path. It's a pity my mother is no longer with us as I am sure she would remember your dad. She died in 2014. My father died in 1998.

Irish women migrants did not have the same issues as the males, as they often had good social skills, had not left a husband and children behind and found interesting non-labouring work in shops, offices and as nurses where they developed good support networks. I have a feeling that if your father was involved in another relationship it would have been with a British woman or a woman with Irish heritage. Most Irish women would have been practising Catholics and would have found out about your dad's history via her networks or through the local priest who would have been on the look out for men who had abandoned families. The priests all had contacts back in Ireland and could check things out for any woman who might be contemplating marriage.

One thing, if your father changed his name once, he could have changed it another time. It is worth noting that he changed it to a common name like Kelly as it would be more difficult to trace than Cushnan.

Peter had worked behind the bar at the Rose & Crown on and off for a few years as a young man:

> Jim was the landlord of the pub. Incidentally, he had barred virtually everyone who was a customer at some time. I am certain that John Kelly was barred at least once. People usually returned a week or so later and would get a nod to say that this was okay. Some did not get the nod and Jim would have very strong quiet words in their ear. I remember Jim once barred three Hull dockers because he couldn't understand a word that they said.
>
> When all the Irish guys were in our pub, they seemed happy so I wouldn't want to paint a miserable picture. But this was not much of a life for anyone at the time. The Irish were poorly educated and spoke

incomprehensible English, although I understood every word even if they had difficulty with my cockney brogue. They dressed in their own fashions, worshipped horses, jockeys and golfers.

Like Sue, Peter tried to explain those Clapham days:

Here's my take on the context for Kelly: there were many Irish men who came to the pub. It was a very very friendly Irish pub that did all the things you would expect – singsongs, the best pint of Guinness in Clapham, after-hours drinking, a place to make acquaintances, plus much interest in horse racing (top priority). Alf was the manager of the betting shop around the corner. He was a very friendly person who once gave me some wonderful advice – 'as a Londoner,' he said, 'I should get out of the smoke and not come back.' Alf said he wished that was what he had done. I took his advice. Leaving London is very hard as you don't have any contact with anywhere else in the country.

Therefore, the Irish men were pretty stuck. They worked on the lump [what we'd call gig economy] and sent money home if they could. They couldn't return to Ireland as this usually meant disgrace in their home as the one who couldn't make it. So we had many Irish people, dressed in worn out secondhand suits, white shirts, ties or work gear and were renting 'digs' with a landlady or a room in a large house with a family.

There were a lot of factories in Clapham in those days, so many worked there or more commonly on building sites. They looked very Irish and were at home in the pub. Nearly all drank Guinness. Perhaps they all could have drank or gambled less, but this was the only social outlet for them. There was little else that they could do.

Sue went on to talk about some of the names I had found among the items in the blue folder. Judy and Vin McManus, who sent a mass card, lived in Clapham Common North.

Judy was a member of the bar staff at the Rose and Crown and her husband was Vin. She worked there for about nine years. They had a few children. I babysat on a number of occasions but don't really remember much. Vin came from the north of Ireland so he may have had some links with your dad. Judy had a sister, Peggy Reilly, and her husband was Hughie. They also came into the pub quite a bit and would have known your dad. They were both first or second generation Irish living in London who had married Irish men. I think Vin was a labourer of some sort but I am not sure.

Peter remembered Judy too:

Judy McManus helped to run the pub during the daytimes Monday to Friday. She had the authority of a landlady when she was around and many would have thought she was just that. She was married to Vin who came from Cavan, I think. Judy was from an English family. Her favourite position was to be firmly planted in the centre of the saloon bar perched on a stool holding court to admirers. Vin was from 'the country'. He spoke little but smiled lots. He had a very broad country accent.

I had sent Sue and Peter copies of the photographs I had found in the blue folder and she was able to help with some of them. She identified the white-haired man on the right of this photograph.

The older man in the photo is Tommy Kennedy who, from my memory, was one of the men who sat in the public bar. I remember him as far back as the early 1960s. He was one of the lost Irish men who used the pub as a place of comfort. The barmaids were very fond of him and used to give him the odd sandwich to go with his pint. I am sure they did the same for your dad. I remember Tommy having Christmas dinner with us on at least one occasion. The wedding picture may have been taken in Ireland. Tommy went back on holidays occasionally.

Peter also remembered Tommy and was able to flesh him out for me:

Tommy Kennedy was fair haired that became white. He was always dressed in a dark suit, white shirt and polished shoes. His hands were small and smooth and he was too thin to cover the shoulders in his jackets. He had a reputation for being good at maths because he could calculate horse odds, betting returns, etc. in an instant. He sat on the edge of the better part of the saloon bar where he could see friends in the public bar but was also strategically placed to offer advice to the saloon bar's well-off crowd and be on the edge of the odd round where he could be gifted a drink. He was a quiet gentleman with a bone dry sense of humour. He was an alcoholic who would never be able, or even wanted, to stop drinking and smoking his Senior Service or Players cigarettes. He was rarely inebriated and was not a binge drinker. He drank halves of Guinness from a thin half-pint glass that had gold lettering to advertise the brand. But hardly anyone drank halves. He'd finish with a gin and tonic and then head home. He was from Galway where his sister owned a bar. I went to visit it when he was alive and was thankful it was closed. It was very dilapidated. He was another Irish man washed up in London incommunicado from the rest of his family. Like most of the Irish men, he did not talk about 'home' or his family and lived alone. Very few returned home. Only one or two went back to the farm they came from.

I think Tommy also lived on Orlando Road, near your father. I once carried him home from the betting shop near the pub. He'd fallen over and cut his head on the gutter. He'd had far too much to drink in the daytime. I took him up the steps to where he lived and his landlady took over. I think that Kelly kept the photo as a memento of Tommy. I liked Tommy lots and he was popular.

Sue commented on a few of the holiday snaps:

Some of the pictures were taken overseas. Many of the Rose and Crown crowd went to Majorca on holiday or Spain. There was a tour operator, Derry Cahill, who worked for Vista Tours (as I did for about 6 months) who used to organise trips for the customers at good prices. The picture of the man on the balcony obviously has his duty-free out. Given the amount he probably travelled with a group of friends. Obviously, you needed a passport for this, so I am not sure if Kelly went with them. The picture of the group [ladies in the carriage] may have been in Palma where you could get carriage rides on the way to dinner.

Both Sue and Peter identified the man standing on the left in the first photograph and sitting on the balcony in the second as 'Scottish' George, a pal of my father's.

Peter added:

[Your father] teamed up with 'Scottish' George, a smallish man who had black, thinning hair kept in position by Brylcreem. He was a shift print worker who almost always wore a black leather coat. Kelly favoured a donkey jacket. Like Kelly, George enjoyed Navy Neaters rum. George would sometimes come to the pub at about midnight with the next morning's *Daily Mirror*.

Commenting on the photograph of the woman, Sue wrote:

The only person that … resembles is Mary English, the wife of Pat English. Many of these women, like Mary, had dreadful lives with their husbands. Marriage had no appeal to me as a young woman from the lives I saw around me.

Peter remembered my father quite clearly:

143

I was told in amazement by my father that he found out who Kelly really was at the funeral. John Kelly, as he was known to us, appears in my memory after 1973. The Rose and Crown was a very busy pub for most of the time. There are many stories that I can remember to do with how the place was run and the things that used to happen. Insofar as John was concerned, he was part of the 'public bar' crowd. There was a dividing wall between the public bar and the saloon bar. The more middle class went to the saloon. Kelly was usually positioned near the public bar door entrance so that he could make occasional forays into the saloon bar. For some reason, most of the customers seemed to stay in the same seats. Regulars had their usual places.

Kelly was always smiling, and would always want to tell you a joke 'Peter, have you heard this one…' and then crack several jokes. I think he was a Guinness man, but he was definitely a rum man and liked Navy Neaters as his choice of drink, particularly during the inevitable after-hours sessions that were very frequent in the pub. He had reddish cheeks, upright white-grey hair and a very large smile. I remember that he was very generous and talkative. So it was easy to have a chat with him. In my memory, he never spoke about Derry. He told me that he was from Belfast and had worked in the merchant navy. If asked about Belfast or his past, he would touch his nose as if to say he had been up to something secretive. I don't think he was ever involved in anything like this, as it was not meant to be taken seriously. I never pursued this as he joked his way out of any serious conversation.

Peter recalled something rather amusing about my father and revealed a talent that surprised me. It's not much of a talent to be honest, but it's a good story.

It was during a fete one summer on Clapham Common. As usual, I was stuck behind the bar serving. But I remember this being a really hot day and everyone was on the Common.

There was a 'welly-wanging' contest set up with a pretty decent prize. I can't remember how much but it was in pounds when they were worth a lot more than they are today. You had to pay an entrance fee. Kelly did this and word got around. It was a joke. He was up against young muscular people. Some of the men took their shirts off to fling the wellies as far as they could. They lifted up the welly and flung it spinning in the air. Wherever it landed, the distance was measured. The last up was Kelly who was supposedly the joke candidate. People were laughing. He took the welly by the heel (not the top), even more laughter, and threw it. It sailed in a straight line through the air and landed miles ahead of the nearest rival. Big cheers. I don't think they did this contest again as Kelly must have known all along that you can throw a welly much further if you hold it

by the heel. Now we all knew. Very
funny.

I am so grateful to Sue and Peter for filling in a lot of the
background to life in Clapham and, particularly, within the
walls of the Rose & Crown. It seems to me that without the
friends my father made and the company he kept, he would
have struggled to survive. Reading between the lines, he
was happy with George, Tommy, Judy McManus and all
the others in his circle. He was in his element. He could
drink and gamble without anyone nagging him because he
was among like-minded drinkers and gamblers. In that
regard, he felt included and welcome.

I am especially grateful to Sue for suggesting a name for
the mystery woman. I have tried every way I can think of to
find a woman named Mary English who was around
Clapham in the 1970s. Unfortunately I've drawn a blank.
But having immersed myself in this story for a long time, I
am convinced that my father had a relationship or
relationships in the twenty-two years since he left his
family in Belfast. Without anything to back it up, I believe
my father and this Mary English had an affair and they had
a son who may have been in the navy. Maybe one day, the
truth will come out about a parallel family, but for now it's
a dead end.

CHAPTER 9: Shaking Hands – An Imagined
Meeting

While researching, writing and thinking about this project to get to know my father, I often wondered what it would be like to meet him. What would I want to say to him? How would I feel? I had been trying to approach this memoir in a very cool, calm, objective way, adhering to the facts I uncovered and trying not to let too much speculation muddy the waters. What I really needed was a way to express my reaction to it all as a sixty-something man, now a husband and a father myself.

The idea nagged away at me until I figured out a method to explore some degree of closure. I decided to dramatise an imagined meeting – me at sixty and him at eighty-nine. What would we talk about, How would I react to him? Would I be ready to forgive, forget and reconcile? Would he be full of remorse or oblivious to the damage he'd caused fifty years earlier when he abandoned his wife and children?

A dramatised meeting also gave me rein to imagine what his voice might have sounded like. I have photographs of him but no idea of the timbre of his voice. His accent would be easy to imagine – broad, hard Belfast – but did he have a deep voice or a soft voice or a gravelly voice or a nasal voice or a shouty voice? Did he swear? And that led me to wonder how he walked? Was it a straight, tidy walk or a pigeon-toed walk or a John Wayne walk or a gangly walk or a mincing walk? So far in this story he has been a silent static character. Now I get to animate him.

So here is my meeting with my father as I imagined it taking place in 2014. There is a high percentage of factual information here but I have allowed myself some dramatic invention. I think the dialogue is plausible. The ending came from my gut. It rings true, to me anyway.

Characters
JOE – 60-year-old Belfast man.
JOHN – eighty-nine-year-old father of JOE.

Joe walks up the gravel path and knocks on the front door of No. 6 Orlando Road, Clapham.

JOE: (*to himself*) You can do this. You can do this. You can do this. Deep breath.

The front door opens

JOE: Hello. I'm Joe.

JOHN: Well, well, come in, come in. It's cold out there.

JOE: Aye, it's a bit nippy.

JOHN: Can I take your coat?

The front door closes

JOE: I'll keep my coat on. I'm not sure how long I'll be here.

JOHN: Suit yourself. Sit down, sit down. Excuse the mess. I've made some tea, or perhaps you'd prefer something a bit stronger.

JOE: Just the tea.

Rattle of teacups.

JOHN: Shaky hands. I suppose I'm a bit nervous.

JOE: I'll pour if you like.

He pours the tea.

JOHN: How did you find me after all these years? I'm glad you did, by the way.

JOE: Oh, it's easy enough these days using the internet to find clues. One thing leads to another and I suppose I got lucky. I sent letters to several addresses but got nothing back, until you phoned me.

JOHN: The internet. Boy, that's some machine. I don't understand it, but it's really not for old guys like me. I always struggled with understanding technology, but it rules the world now. I never even mastered how to get coffee out of a machine without spilling it. (*pause*) Well, thanks for finding me and for coming to see me. It was a big surprise to hear from you – from anyone over there. I don't know how we'll get on but we'll see how it goes. (*pause*) So, where do we start?

JOE: I have so many questions and I'm hoping you have most of the answers.

JOHN: Fire away. Custard cream?

JOE: (*sharply*) No. I didn't come here for tea and biscuits.

JOHN: You seem a bit on edge, son.

JOE: Please don't call me that.

JOHN: It's just an expression.

JOE: I might have been your son over fifty years ago but you drew a line under that. I'm here to find things out.

JOHN: Like to get straight to the point, eh? Over fifty years. That would make you ...

JOE: Sixty. I turned sixty earlier this year.

JOHN: My God. Sixty. You can stop a lot of things but not time. Not the clock. I'm eighty-nine.

JOE: I know. (*pause*) Why did you leave?

JOHN: It's complicated.

JOE: Well, uncomplicate it.

JOHN: Before we get to that, why didn't you shake my hand at the front door?

JOE: I'm not ready for that yet.

JOHN: It's just common courtesy. But no matter. Why did I leave, you ask. It's ... it's ... difficult to remember clearly.

JOE: It was 1960. I was six.

JOHN: Aye, 1960. That's about right. You see, your mother and me got married in the late forties. It wasn't long before kids started appearing and money started to get tight. It was expensive running a family, especially in those days.

JOE: You wasting money on booze and cigarettes didn't help. Throwing it down the drain at the bookies wasn't too clever either.

JOHN: A wee smoke and a drink back then was part of a working man's life. A flutter now and again on the horses was part of our entertainment. It was different then. Men and women had different roles. We all knew our places.

JOE: Why did you leave?

JOHN: I couldn't cope. It was as simple as that. Pressure. I couldn't cope with the pressure.

JOE: Pressure? What about the pressure your wife was left with? Seven young children. Did we mean nothing to you? Did she mean nothing to you?

JOHN: I couldn't cope. The easiest thing was to get out of there. I knew what I was leaving behind. I'm not proud of it. If I'd stayed, it would have done my head in. (*pause*) But what can I do about it now?

JOE: I remember the night you left. You had a battered old brown suitcase. You walked out the front door. I don't think you even looked back. I saw you from the window standing at the bus stop. The bus came and you were gone.

JOHN: It wasn't an easy decision, you know. Times were hard back then. Belfast wasn't a good place for work then.

JOE: Where did you go?

JOHN: First to Liverpool, then I headed here to Clapham and stayed for a few years in a bedsit above a pub. Then I got into a relationship with the landlord's sister. She was in London on a visit from Portsmouth. One thing led to another and I moved in with her down there.

JOE: Did you marry her?

JOHN: No. I was still married to your mother. (*pause*) If you're looking for a bombshell, I suppose here it comes. (*pause*) We had a child, a wee boy.

JOE: What?

JOHN: A son. I made up my mind to tell you everything you wanted to know – the good, the bad and the ugly, as far as I can remember things. He was a lovely child.

JOE: Was?

JOHN: Michael. He was seven when he was knocked down on the way to school. Died instantly. December 1976. A few days before Christmas. (*sniffs loudly*) Broke my heart. It's still broken. (*sniffs*)

JOE: I'm having trouble taking this in. In fifty years, not once did you get in touch with your seven children in Belfast – nothing at Christmas, nothing on birthdays, nothing. We were the family that never was while you were carving out a new life over here.

JOHN: I can't justify it. But that's what happened. When I left, I thought I'd go away for a short while, make a bit of money and then come back home. But time got the better of me. On a couple of occasions I rang up to book a ferry but I put the phone down. Stupid, stupid. You look a bit pale. Do you want a beer or something?

JOE: No, I don't want a drink. I'm trying to make sense of this.

JOHN: A wee boy died. There's no sense to it.

JOE: It's sad, very sad. But I'm trying to untangle a lot of things here.

JOHN: Tell me about your brothers and sisters.

JOE: Six of us are still alive. Paul was killed in an accident in 1974, not long after driving his lorry off the Cairnryan ferry. I don't really want to drag the rest of them into the conversation. This is between you and me as far as I am concerned. All you need to know is they are all doing fine in their own ways.

JOHN: And what about you?

JOE: I'm retired now. I spent forty years in the supermarket game, running shops and other things. The chance came for early retirement, so I grabbed it. Supermarkets are a young person's thing.

JOHN: I hate them. The wee shop on the corner serves my needs. (*pause*) How's your mother?

JOE: She died last year.

JOHN: Oh, holy God. I wasn't expecting that.

JOE: Don't go all sad and sorry. You didn't give a damn about her.

JOHN: (*angrily*) Don't you dare say that to me. You don't know the truth of anything that happened. I'm sad about it and I *am* sorry.

JOE: (*raising his voice*) The truth? The truth? You wouldn't know the truth if it slapped you in the face. It's you that doesn't know the truth about all that hardship back then. You abandoned our mother, left her to scramble around for a wee bit of extra money here and there to beef up her family allowance. You walked away and didn't bat an eyelid.

JOHN: (*quietly*) She was in my heart and in my head. All of you were.

JOE: (*shouting now*) Don't give me any of that old pluck. You were selfish and thoughtless and useless. I'd love to punch you in the guts but you probably don't have any.

JOHN: (*shouting*) I can still fight, boy. I'm still handy. I can throw a punch. Give me some respect.

JOE: (*shouting*) Ha! Respect? Respect? That's something people earn and you're way off the mark there. (*pause*) I wish you'd died a long time ago.

JOHN: (*angrily*) Get the hell out of here. Get out. I'm not having anybody speak to me like that. Go on, piss off.

Pause

JOE: (*quietly*) Look, I'm sorry. I know this is hard for both of us. I just want to know some things, that's all. Some of the things will be hard to stomach but I need to know them. I need to hear them.

JOHN: (*whispering*) Okay. Okay.

JOE: What kind of work did you do when you left?

JOHN: Well, I took the boat to Liverpool and got talking to a guy who owned a haulage business. He said he was always looking for drivers and he offered me a job. I got some digs near the docks and drove for him for a few months – until I got sick of the hours and the miles. So I upped sticks and headed for London.

JOE: Did you ever think of sending some money back to Mum?

JOHN: In all honesty, my head was about surviving myself. Now don't start but that's the way I felt at the time. I found a bedsit near the Arsenal ground and then bought myself a cheap suit, a couple of shirts and ties. I fancied an office job. Eventually at the Labour Exchange, I found a job as a tailor's assistant, a cloth cutter. That was steady work. Clean work.

JOE: What was your first Christmas like away from Belfast, away from us?

JOHN: It was a bit strange, to tell you the truth. I didn't know many people. I just sat in my room with one bar of the electric fire on. I opened a couple of tins of soup and a

156

few beers during the day. I didn't own a TV but I did have a radio. It kept me company.

JOE: Did you miss us?

JOHN: I did. I felt a bit sorry for myself.

JOE: But you got over it.

JOHN: I'd made my bed. I was alone because I chose to be. Christmas came and went. It was no big deal. (*pause*) What about you? Did you miss me?

JOE: I don't remember. I know in all the years you weren't there, my mother always made Christmases and birthdays special for us. We were young enough to ignore all that adult stuff.

JOHN: So you didn't miss me.

JOE: No. All we cared about were our toys, sweets and comics. You were out of sight and out of mind. I have no idea what Mum was thinking but she never showed any sign of misery or unhappiness.

JOHN: Do you remember anything about me? Apart from Christmas, I mean.

JOE: My two memories …

JOHN: Only two?

JOE: My two memories of you are sausages burning, and shaving soap.

JOHN: Sausages burning? What the hell was that about?

JOE: You allowed sausages to burn in the pan one night when you were drunk.

JOHN: I don't remember that one. What about the shaving soap?

JOE: It was horrible.

JOHN: It was probably cheap rubbish.

JOE: It certainly wasn't like an Old Spice or a Brut smell, that's for sure. (*pause*) I can still remember the strong smell of that shaving soap from the few times you hugged me. It was a thick smell, like the old carbolic soap we used to get.

JOHN: It's funny what people remember. Sausages and soap.

JOE: What do you remember about me?

JOHN: It's hard to remember much about those days. It's half a century ago.

JOE: I know, but isn't there anything you remember about me?

JOHN: I could make a few things up just to kid you but you're not in a kidding mood. I'm sorry, son – er, Joe – it's all a blur to me. I remember Paul because he was the eldest. But then I struggle. (*sighs*) Are you sure you won't take off your coat? You'll feel the benefit of it when you go outside.

JOE: No, I'm fine thanks. Why are you still shaking? It looks like a bit more than nerves to me.

JOHN: Look, if you must know, the doctor checked me over when I last went for a blood pressure test. He said it's something called essential tremors, common in old people but he said he couldn't discount early stages of Parkinson's. Essential tremors. Essential. Sounds as if there's no choice in the matter. I'd call them bloody nuisance tremors – old bugger's shaky mitts.

JOE: I'm sorry to hear that. (*pause*) You live on your own, don't you?

JOHN: Aye. It's been that way for a lot of years now.

JOE: Kind of ironic, don't you think?

JOHN: What's that supposed to mean?

JOE: Well, you had a chance to be part of a big family – home comforts, your kids, a loving wife – and it's all come to this. Lonely and alone.

JOHN: Sometimes I'm lonely but other times I like it. I can look after myself, although it's getting harder at my age. I don't hear or see people for days. That's one reason I was glad of your letter and our wee chat on the phone. But I don't want your pity. I don't want any pity.

JOE: No chance of that. I don't – won't pity you.

JOHN: Are your brothers and sisters all hard like you?

JOE: They can speak for themselves if they want to. We're not hard people by nature but what you did affected us all.

JOHN: I suppose I have to accept that.

JOE: What was the name of the landlord's sister?

JOHN: Mary English.

JOE: How long were you together?

JOHN: Oh, about eight years. It was good most of the time but I made a bollocks of it in the end. I wasn't pulling my weight with the housekeeping and when Michael was born, well, everything felt strained. Mary didn't really want kids, you see. Neither did I, to tell you the truth. No offence.

JOE: We've gone way past offence. You couldn't keep it in your trousers, was that it?

JOHN: (*loudly*) Now, don't talk to me like that. We all know how it works in the bedroom. We don't always think things through but we know how it works.

JOE: You had seven kids back in Belfast. If you didn't want children, why did you keep …

JOHN: Ach, it's a Catholic thing. No frenchies allowed. But a man has needs, urges and, well, we all know how it works.

JOE: Sitting here, right now, listening to you makes me sick. I don't know what I was expecting but I'm beginning to regret finding you. I should have let things lie. You

160

disgust me. All this is so matter-of-fact to you. It happened, you shrug your shoulders and that's it.

JOHN: (*shouting*) I can't help the way you feel about me. I know you don't like me or what I did and I can't justify it or defend it. It happened and I've – we've – got to live with it. It can't be undone.

Pause

JOE: (*calmly*) My mother was the greatest woman I've ever known, full of courage and optimism and faith. She was thrown in at the deep end. D'you know, she even had to ask friends and neighbours for money just to feed her kids. You forced her to beg.

JOHN: I didn't know that.

JOE: Why would you?

JOHN: It must have been hard, right enough.

JOE: Is that all you can say – it must have been hard?

JOHN: What can I do? What can I do now?

JOE: (*sarcastically*) Nothing. Nothing at all.

Pause

JOHN: Can I make you a wee sandwich? I've got crusty rolls and meat paste.

JOE: No thanks. But you go ahead if you're hungry.

JOHN: I'll be all right for a bit.

JOE: You said the Portsmouth thing didn't work out. How did you end up here, in this house?

JOHN: After Michael was killed, Mary and me struggled on for a year or so. What with her death and all, the strain just got worse and I did what I suppose I'm good at – I walked out and moved back to London. A friend of a friend owns this house and he lets me have it for not a lot of rent. He wants to do it up and sell it eventually, but he isn't ready to spend the money yet. He reckons I'm not long for this world, so he's showing me a kindness.

JOE: I've been thinking about this a lot. In over fifty years it stands to reason that you must have had more than one relationship with women.

JOHN: What are you getting at?

JOE: Are there any more kids out there?

JOHN: Well, that's a bit personal.

JOE: Personal is what this is all about.

JOHN: I've had a healthy share of women down the years but I've always tried to be careful. As far as I know, there are no more children. Why? Is it important to you?

JOE: (*agitated*) Can't you see? Are you thick? Can't you hear yourself? Years, decades fly by and there are big gaps in my knowledge about you. Who are you? What are you? Why did you piss off? Where did you go? Who were you with? And how the hell did you get away with it?

162

JOHN: Get away with what?

JOE: Abandoning your family. Neglect.

JOHN: It was wrong, very, very wrong, but there's no law against it. I told you before, I can't justify any of it. I just couldn't handle the pressure. God knows, if I'd stayed I might have made things worse. I might have jumped off a bridge.

JOE: (*annoyed*) There's still time.

JOHN: For a little forgiveness?

JOE: No, to throw yourself off a bridge.

JOHN: I should've seen that one coming.

JOE: I only half mean it. Can I make you a sandwich now?

JOHN: Aye, that would be nice.

JOE: I'll clear these tea things away.

JOHN: Just leave them in the sink. I'll do them later.

FADE

In the living room of JOHN's house

JOHN: That was a nice sandwich. Thank you. So where are you living these days?

JOE: Nottingham.

JOHN: Any family?

JOE: My wife and two grown-up sons.

JOHN: What are their names?

JOE: No, I'm not going down this road. I don't want to share my family with you. You don't deserve to know about them. You're probably not really interested anyway.

JOHN: I'm trying to put pieces into the jigsaw too, you know. I'm eighty-nine. I'm entitled, at least in my own head, to look back, to take stock, good and bad.

JOE: That's your business. I'm not ready, and probably never will be, to let you get close to me or my family. I can't stop you wishing and dreaming and analysing your life. But you are not part of mine.

JOHN: So why are you here? I mean, really.

JOE: When Mum was ill, I started to compile a book of thoughts, messages and poetry about her life and mine. It gave me a chance to get stuff out of my system. I wrote about you too and how little you meant to me and the rest of the family. When I was remembering the past, I became curious about you – not in any sentimental way, just curious about how you'd ended up.

JOHN: If you wrote things about me, I must mean something.

JOE: Ha! Believe what you want.

JOHN: I have an inkling you care.

JOE: Don't flatter yourself. I wrote about the callous way you just walked out. Now I look around here and I see an untidy house, a dirty kitchen. God knows what the bathroom is like. And when was the last time you had a good wash? There's a bad smell in here.

JOHN: Now, wait a wee minute …

JOE: On the sideboard there, an ashtray full of used Bic razors.

JOHN: Somebody from the pub drops them through the letterbox every once in a while. Have you seen the price of razor blades?

JOE: If it was me, I'd rather grow a beard than accept charity like that.

JOHN: Well, it's not you, is it?

JOE: It's pitiful. In the kitchen – one pan, a kettle, one mug, one plate. Here you are at eighty-nine and the things you own wouldn't fill half a pillowcase. Just pitiful.

JOHN: You forgot the two china cups and saucers on the tray and the wee milk jug. (*pause*) Look, I don't need things. I don't want things. This is me. This is my house. This is what I am. If you don't like how my house looks or how I smell, tough.

JOE: You could have had a life with a family back in Belfast, home comforts, love even. You could have tried harder to cope with that pressure you keep going on about.

My mother managed the hardship. You could have tried harder. (*sniffs loudly*)

JOHN: Are you crying, son?

JOE: Oh, get lost. You have no idea. (*angrily*) Do you want to know what you missed? Do you want a few gaps filled in? When you left in 1960, I was in primary school. Five years later, I was in grammar school. I got four O-levels. In 1971, I got my first job as an office clerk. In 1973, I started my career as a shop manager. In 1980, I got married. In 1984, we had a son. In 1986, we had another son. In 1992, I got my Open University degree. My life went on without you. No hugs, no pats on the back, no congratulations or well dones, nothing. You missed out on so many things that might just have made you a better man. But I can't help thinking, now that I've met you, that if you'd stayed we would have been worse off. Maybe God was doing a good deed on that day cutting you out of our lives for good reason.

Pause

JOHN: I cried at the bus stop that day. Something hit me on that short walk to the bus stop. It bothered me because I haven't cried before or since.

JOE: Not even when your son died?

JOHN: Not even then. I was too angry to cry. Does that make sense? I wanted to find the driver and tear him apart. I didn't, of course. I just looked at my wee dead Michael and felt desperately sad. But no tears. I don't know why. People around me were bawling their eyes out but I felt like stone.

JOE: Something about that doesn't surprise me.

JOHN: Tell me about Paul.

JOE: Paul was a lorry driver. He used transport goods to Scotland and England on the Belfast-Cairnryan ferry. On his last trip, his lorry went out of control a mile or so down the road from the docks and he was killed instantly. He was only twenty-six.

JOHN: God almighty.

JOE: That's nearly forty years ago. Devastated us.

JOHN: I'm sure it did. Too young. Far too young. What about the girls?

JOE: They're all fine. They stepped up when Mum needed twenty-four-hour care. They worked out a rota of shifts and made sure she was well looked after at home. Three angels. My younger brother is well settled with his family. My older brother is somewhere in or near London.

JOHN: The way you talk about them makes me want to see them as they are now.

JOE: Well, it's unlikely you'll ever see them in the flesh. I know they have no interest in you. But I do have two photographs. Black and white. This one is the only photograph of the entire Cushnan family – well, almost all of it you, Mum and six children. Kevin wasn't born yet. Here.

JOHN: My God. I can hardly see it for my hands shaking.

JOE: Hold it with both hands.

JOHN: Aye, that's better.

JOE: We think that picture was taken at home around 1957. See how happy we all look?

JOHN: It's a happy group right enough. I'd forgotten what you all looked like. Your mother looks good.

JOE: Is it hard to say 'my wife looks good'.

JOHN: Ach, stopping playing with words. Around 1958, you say. Your mother, er, my wife …

JOE: Say her name, for God's sake.

JOHN: Rita. A handsome family. You might have to help me decide who's who.

JOE: No, I'm not going to do that. All you need to know today is that I am the startled kid in the middle. If you can't recall the others, too bad. A couple of years later you were gone. Out of the picture in more ways than one.

JOHN: Seeing everybody together brings it all back. I felt pressure trying to stay afloat with work and money. But I look at that photograph – smiling, happy faces – and there's not a hint of pressure. I must have been – must be – a terrible man. Here.

JOE: You can keep the photo. I had a copy made for you. If you want it, that is.

JOHN: Oh, yes, yes. Thank you. I'll treasure it.

JOE: I hope you will. Pin it to the wall to remind you what you lost, what you threw away.

JOHN: I missed so many things, didn't I? Birthdays, holidays, Christmases, school reports, engagements, weddings, grandchildren ... how many grandchildren are there?

JOE: Twelve. Eight boys and four girls.

JOHN: Jeez. (*sniffs loudly*)

JOE: That's the kind of stuff you can never get back. It's lost forever. And then there was the teasing at school because I only had one parent.

JOHN: If you're trying to make me feel more guilty than I ever have, you're doing a great job.

JOE: Good. (*pause*) You know, the strangest thing is that I thought I'd enjoy this more, watching you squirm and try to defend yourself. But it's just making me more miserable. Still, you need to know some of this stuff and when I've gone and you're alone with your thoughts, regrets might just eat away at your insides.

JOHN: You're a nasty piece of work when you put your mind to it.

JOE: I was talking to someone about how best to handle this and the advice was to be direct, straight and blunt. There's no time for a softly-softly approach.

169

JOHN: You mentioned two photographs.

JOE: Here's the other one. It's your wedding day.

JOHN: Lord God almighty, would you look at that.

JOE: I wrote the date on the back. Sixteenth of September 1947.

JOHN: I remember where it was taken. A photographer's studio in Belfast. Now what was the name of it? Ginley's? Garvey's? Ach, my mind's going.

JOE: You were both around twenty-two.

JOHN: Your mother, her sister Sheila and cousin Marie. And there's Gerry Savage, the best man. God, I'd forgotten him completely.

JOE: He was always the mystery man in the photo.

JOHN: We were workmates and drinking pals. I was best man at his wedding, so he returned the favour.

JOE: So how do you feel when you look at that picture?

JOHN: It's like I'm looking at another world. It's getting on for seventy years ago, but it brings a lot of things back. We were only youngsters getting married, full of love and hope for the future. Just two years after the war. God knows the world needed hope after all that carry on. Can I keep this one too?

JOE: It's yours.

JOHN: I really appreciate these memories, even though you might not believe it.

JOE: Right, well, I'd better be going.

JOHN: Stay a bit longer.

JOE: I have a train to catch, but I suppose a few more minutes won't do any harm.

JOHN: I could make more tea, or whatever you want.

JOE: No, I'm fine. (*pause*) What about you? Do you have any photographs of your life after you left?

JOHN: A few, but not many. Have a look in that drawer over there. There's a shoebox of bits and pieces.

Sound of a cabinet drawer opening, some shuffling of contents and the drawer closing.

JOE: I'll let you rummage.

JOHN: Let's see. It's been a long time since I looked in this box. (*frustrated*) Damn it. These shaking hands of mine are a bloody nuisance.

JOE: Do you want me to do it?

JOHN: No, I'll be all right. Ah, here's one of Mary and me at the seaside not long after I moved down there.

JOE: Pretty.

JOHN: She was indeed. Nice girl, but a bit fiery when riled. Here's one of me on a bike to somewhere or other. And, Lord help me, there's wee Michael.

JOE: He looks sweet.

JOHN: Oh he was, he was. He could wrap me round his little finger with a cute smile or a pretend sad face.

JOE: Eight children.

JOHN: What?

JOE: You had eight children.

JOHN: I know that. I know.

JOE: And you only seem emotional about one.

JOHN: Ach, he was a wee boy.

JOE: We were all wee once.

JOHN: I'll never win with you.

JOE: No, you won't.

JOHN: You're a desperate man.

JOE: I'll bet if I rummaged in that shoebox or in those drawers or anywhere in the house, you wouldn't have a single memento of us.

JOHN: I suppose you're right. I think I started out with a few things but they got lost along the way. I told you, I don't need things.

JOE: And you didn't need our family.

JOHN: Look, Joe, I'll be dead in the not too distant future. It stands to reason. What I could do with is your forgiveness.

JOE: No, no. That's not going to happen.

JOHN: A little humanity for an old man. Is that too much to ask?

JOE: Yes, far too much. No, no, it's not going to happen.

Pause

JOHN: Did your mother – did Rita get a good send-off?

JOE: She lived in the same house for nigh on sixty years and everybody knew her. When we carried the coffin outside, we couldn't believe the crowd that had gathered. Hundreds of people – friends, neighbours all turned out that morning. And it was freezing. The church was packed to the rafters. The priest said he'd never seen anything like it. (*pause*) Yes, she got a good send-off.

JOHN: I wish I'd known.

JOE: Why? You wouldn't have come over, would you?

JOHN: No, probably not. But I'd like to have known and maybe have said a wee prayer for her soul.

JOE: (*agitated*) Would you stop it! Just stop it! I can't stomach your feeble attempts at giving a toss.

JOHN: (*angrily*) You can't stop me from thinking and feeling anyway I like. You're not the emotional police.

JOE: I've been around long enough to know a fraud.

JOHN: God help me. I can say nothing, think nothing, feel nothing, do nothing without you jumping down my throat.

JOE: That's because you are nothing.

JOHN: You know, when I got your letter and we spoke on the phone, there was none of this bitterness in your voice. I had hopes that we would have a friendly chat about the old days and a bit of a catch-up about our lives. I even had an inkling that there might just be a wee hint of reconciliation. Even the worst of enemies can find common ground somewhere. Look at the characters running Northern Ireland now – once enemies, now working together.

JOE: After a fashion. Old wounds haven't healed there and they haven't even begun to heal here in this room.

JOHN: Surely we can work out the past. After all, we're of the same blood.

JOE: I can't change that, sadly.

JOHN: Have you never made mistakes?

JOE: I haven't abandoned my family.

JOHN: I didn't ask you that.

JOE: Of course I've made bloody mistakes, but that's not relevant.

JOHN: I'm just trying to make a point. We're all human. Were youse okay during the Troubles?

JOE: Are you for real? There you go again, pretending to care. We all lived to tell our tales.

JOHN: Except poor Paul.

JOE: That had nothing to do with the Troubles.

JOHN: I know. I know.

JOE: One time, we were lying on the floor for protection from a gunman who was outside our window. He was a sniper shooting at soldiers, using our wall to hide.

JOHN: I saw plenty of stuff like that on the news.

JOE: Mum started to pray loudly, Our Fathers and Hail Marys to give us comfort, to kinda shield us from the shooting. She prayed hard, almost begging God to protect us from harm.

JOHN: Religion. Not everyone's cup of tea.

JOE: She found great strength in her faith. Sometimes she had to dig deep to trust God just to survive. It was more than her cup of tea – it was crucial to her.

JOHN: I gave religion up years ago. Couldn't see the point of it.

JOE: You gave up. What a surprise! Look, I really must get going.

JOHN: I'll walk to the Tube station with you.

JOE: You don't have to.

JOHN: I know, but I go out for a short walk most days. I'll just get my anorak.

FADE

Joe and John walk along Orlando Road.

JOHN: I like this street. It's away from the mayhem of the High Street. And I love trees. If you have trees you have birds too. Singing away. And squirrels, busy doing not much. It's not the country but it's nice.

JOE: When did you start using the walking stick?

JOHN: A couple of years ago. I could feel my knees getting a bit weak. I found this oul thing in a charity shop. They only wanted a pound for it. What with my old bones and shaking hands, I'm feeling a bit worn out. (*pause*) Did you get what you came for?

JOE: I suppose so.

JOHN: I enjoyed it. It was great to find out a few things and to see you again. Did I look the way you thought I'd look?

JOE: I had an idea from that family snap and just figured you'd have white hair and a lot of wrinkles. I wasn't sure if you'd be fat or thin. But, you've kept your weight in check.

JOHN: That's just an act of God what with the amount of food and drink I've shifted in my time. Get to a certain age and your appetite changes. You don't need as much of anything to survive.

JOE: There is one thing.

JOHN: What's that?

JOE: Did you ever hit my mother?

JOHN: No, not really.

JOE: What the hell does 'not really' mean?

JOHN: I mean I didn't do anything on purpose.

JOE: So you did hit her.

JOHN: I might have pushed her when she nagged a bit too much. But I don't remember hitting her.

JOE: There's talk you did.

JOHN: What talk?

JOE: From people who were close to her, people she confided in.

JOHN: I didn't hit her. I have no memory of anything like that.

JOE: They say that's why you left. You hit her once too often and she told you to get out of the house. It was her choice, not yours.

JOHN: It was my decision, not your mother's. I told you. I couldn't handle the pressure of trying to keep afloat.

JOE: I heard you hit her more than once when she would almost have to beg you for housekeeping money. But there wasn't any. You'd pissed it up the wall of the pub.

JOHN: She had family allowance. Claiming for seven kids was a nice wee earner, you know.

Joe grabs John's coat lapels and they scuffle on the street.

JOE: (*menacingly*) You're an evil bastard. Is that why you kept at it? To have as many kids as possible to make money?

JOHN: (*shouting*) Let go of my coat. Let go of my coat. Get your hands off me.

JOE: Okay, okay. I'm sorry. But can't you hear yourself sometimes? You sound so cold about things, so matter-of-fact.

JOHN: Things were different back then. Husbands went to work. Wives stayed at home. Their job was to have kids, raise kids, cook, clean and keep their opinions to themselves. That was the way of things were. Everybody knew their place.

JOE: She must have been miserable being married to you. But, you know what, she never showed any of that to us. She looked after every one of us. *We* were her place and she didn't walk away.

JOHN: I was prepared for a lot of hard words but I wasn't expecting you to attack me physically.

JOE: I'm sorry. It's out of character, but you do say some stupid things.

JOHN: All I'm trying to do is explain as much as I can. The 1950s was a different era altogether.

JOE: In any age, a man who hits a woman isn't worth spit.

JOHN: I didn't hit her. As far as I can remember, I didn't hit your mother.

JOE: As far as you can remember. Alcohol amnesia. They say you would come home drunk most nights.

JOHN: Who are these people? Who are these gossips?

JOE: The names don't matter but they were sober at the time and still have clear memories. They're more credible than you'll ever be.

JOHN: The names matter to me, destroying my good …

JOE: Good name? Is that what you were about to say? Good name?

JOHN: I have to defend some of the things being hurled at me. I might be bad in your eyes, but I'm not all bad.

JOE: I'll have to take your word for that.

JOHN: Haven't you had any sense of me – I mean me, now, today? Is there anything good you see? Anything good you can say?

JOE: I see a sad old man who rewrites history, forgets things when it suits him and who doesn't show an ounce of remorse. Except for his dead illegitimate son.

JOHN: Now just be very careful there. Don't use my wee Michael as a pawn in this game. I knew him. I didn't really have any connection with you, your brothers and sisters. It's not anybody else's fault but mine. But don't bring that wee boy into any hatred you have for me. Even if he was alive, he doesn't deserve it. This is not his fight.

JOE: No. You're right. It's not his fight. It's my fight. I've had you nagging in the back of my mind for years. I can't get rid of you. And now that I've met you, I have new images in my head, more stuff to carry round, more baggage to drag through the rest of my life. What was I thinking coming here? What the hell was I thinking? I should have let your memory fade away but no, I had to track you down.

JOHN: Aw, come on …

JOE: Three memories.

JOHN: Three?

JOE: Sausages, shaving soap and shite.

JOHN: (*sighing*) We're a lost cause.

JOE: You're the lost cause.

JOHN: Is there anyway we can restore this relationship?

JOE: There is no relationship. There never was and there never will be. Don't you get that?

JOHN: I rest my case. Lost cause.

JOE: Who'll be at your funeral?

JOHN: What?

JOE: Who'll make your funeral arrangements and attend your funeral?

JOHN: I don't know and, frankly, I don't care. I might just peg out at home and lie there until somebody breaks down the door. By that stage, who cares?

JOE: Doesn't that bother you?

JOHN: Why should it bother me? When you're dead, that's it. You're gone. They can throw me in a skip for all I care.

JOE: That sums you up. Not giving a damn.

JOHN: Look, I think we better leave it there. We're getting nowhere. It's just turning into a slanging match. We are what we are, good or bad and nothing's going to change that.

JOE: Goodbye, then.

JOHN: Good luck to you. (*pause*) Are you going to shake my hand now?

Longer pause

JOE: No. I don't want you to get any impression that I like you or forgive you or care about you in any way. There's a river of sorrow and disappointment between us in a fifty-four-year chasm and no bridge for us to meet in the middle. So, no handshake, no hug and no love lost.

JOHN: Please, son. Please don't leave it like this. (*sobbing*) I can't fix the past but I can be part of your future. All I need is a little forgiveness for my sins.

JOE: Goodbye, Mister John Kelly.

JOHN: Mister Kelly? I'm John Cushnan. I'm your daddy.

JOE: Goodbye.

END

Yes, I really do believe I would have been that decisive, that cold!

EPILOGUE

I started this project with the intention of staying focused on my father's story. He left, he went missing, he turned up dead. It would make a very slim volume, I thought. But as I explored it, I found myself considering not just this runaway man but also the people he left behind and what effect his actions had on them. I began to wonder about his upbringing, his family and social background in Belfast. What shaped him? What unravelled him? What made him buckle under the pressures of being husband and father? What made him the villain of our family's story?

And that, in turn, led me to think the same way about my mother. What was her story? What kind of a girl was she? Where did she find the courage and resilience to step up in the way she did when the front door closed behind my father in 1960? What made her the true star of this story and how did she become the greatest woman I have ever known? As I progressed with my research, my mother's heroism was worth far more than the couple of sentences I had planned.

Inevitably it brought me to me. I felt it was necessary to include a fair amount of autobiographical details to depict my life with an absent father and to show how he wasn't really necessary in my upbringing. He would have been a big influence on me had he stayed, but who knows what kind of influence that would have been.

Family history is a subject that requires time, patience, persistence and, in a case such as this, a liking for detective stories. It can be that exciting and frustrating. The sheer exhilaration of finding a brand new piece of relevant information has been one of the joys of this whole experience.

What surprised me was how emotional I became at some of the things I discovered. Death certificates particularly made me choke a little as I stopped to reflect on when and how people died. Researching and writing this memoir has been an uneasy mixture of satisfaction, sadness, frustration and challenge. I wish I had been an avid diarist. Had I been one, it would have saved a lot of time digging around and trying to remember details and dates.

Kenneth Williams's diaries – forty-three years' worth – were published in 1993.[20] They are a treasure trove of wit, wisdom and wickedness, of happiness, sadness and brutal honesty. But it is the final entry that resonates most with me as I wrap up this project on my family's history: 'Oh, what's the bloody point?'

I have spent many hours and a lot of money travelling around the country, searching for information and writing it all down and I have often sat back and thought: what's the bloody point? Is it worth the effort?

I tell myself it's for the Cushnans of the future so that they might know some family history. It's also for me because I wanted to know the answers to a lot of nagging questions. But ultimately, it's for my mother. It's a celebration of her life and an acknowledgement of what a heroic job she did in keeping us all together. She's the bloody point.

So now that it's over, what have I learned and am I a better man for it? I've certainly learned a lot from the graft of doing research. I have discovered many things I did not know about my parents, grandparents and those a little further back. I'll leave it to others to say whether I'm a better man.

---

[20] *The Kenneth Williams Diaries*. ed. Russell Davies (London: HarperCollins, 1993).

As for John Cushnan from Belfast who became John Kelly from Derry and then became John Cushnan again in his grave, the words 'abhor', 'detest', 'loathe', 'dislike', 'despise' have all made guest appearances in my thoughts even if they didn't quite make it on to paper. I began this memoir with a quote from the film, *I Never Sang for My Father*: 'I hate him. And I hate to hate him.' But at the end, the word I will settle for is 'coward'.

Finally, it wouldn't be me if I didn't squeeze one more Western reference into this story. *The Searchers*, starring John Wayne, tells the story of a Civil War veteran and his troubled quest to find his kidnapped niece. Its theme song, 'Ride Away', captures something of the reasons for my own quest:

> What makes a man to wander?
> What makes a man to roam?
> What makes a man leave bed and board
> And turn his back on home?

Will I ever forgive my father? As the John Wayne character in the film says several times, 'That'll be the day.'

POSTSCRIPT: Some Notes on Researching

Family History

I had the blue folder of my fathers bits and pieces back in
the early 1980s, when I really should have started to
research my father's 'missing' years. But back then it
would have been a real slog to find out almost anything
about him. It would also have required considerable time
because, pre-internet, pre-Google and all the other online
resources, progress would have been limited and slow as a
tortoise.

It was still a formidable task thirty years later when I did
actually start my research. I had watched many episodes of
Who Do You Think You Are? and was under the impression
that the process was simple: just dig around a bit, find a
few experts, seek out some archive documents and
everything would fall into place. But I later found out that
each episode of that show can take up to a year to complete
as a crack team of researchers pull the story together,
allowing the celebrity relatively easy access to relevant
material.

As I was my one and only researcher, I soon found out
that tracing family history is a roller-coaster of excitement
and frustration with many diversions, obstacles and solid
brick walls en route. But I found the whole experience
addictive. It was exhilarating to unearth new facts and,
particularly, to communicate with people who knew my
father.

After scrutinising the contents of the blue folder, I made
my family aware of what I was planning to do and
encouraged them to recall their own stories about my father

and mother. Every memory, small or large, was important me. Many seemingly minor details can lead to bigger things. Even now, as I draw this project to close, occasional nuggets still emerge. If you want to investigate your family history, ask family members for their perspectives and always, always take notes – in a notebook, I might add, because scraps of paper, backs of receipts and old envelopes, just end up in a jumble or, worse, get lost along the way. It's even better to record conversations with family, friends and contacts, if they are happy for you to do it. Listening to a real voice telling a real story gives it all a wonderful humanity. Whatever your method of accumulating information, be disciplined in this regard.

The next source for me, and all hail the internet, was the 1911 Irish Census via the National Archives of Ireland. What a treasure trove of fascinating information it holds: addresses, names of household occupants, ages, relationships to the head of the household, religion, all sorts of wonderful details. And if that isn't enough, a click takes you to the actual handwritten version of the household's census return. I could see my great-grandfather's and my grandfather's writing style and their signatures.

Another area of valuable information was the Public Records Office. I the visited Public Records Office of Northern Ireland (PRONI) in Belfast a couple of times. PRONI holds a ton of archives, so it's important to write down a list of questions, dates and other relevant information to enable the archivists there help you find what you are looking for. The General Register Office (GRO), Belfast, was where I went to find birth, death and marriage certificates online. If perusing in their building on their computers, it is a free service. But if you want copies, there is a charge. So my advice is to pick and choose the certificates that are most important to your lines of research. These certificates give specific dates, addresses and occupations among other things, and often one fact or clue can lead to another. One of the striking things that a death certificate reveals, for example, is cause of death, and that can sometimes be linked to housing and work conditions particularly among the working class. On some certificates, it was an emotional shock to read of past relatives who had died quite young. The GRO also has a helpful team to assist.

A particularly fascinating resource was the Newspaper Library, part of Belfast Central Library. It holds a vast array of hard copy and microfiche reels of just about every Northern Ireland newspaper since the eighteenth century. Yet another helpful team processes your request and heads for the storage area to seek out whatever newspaper you want. There is a lot of information to be gleaned from the obituary columns. The newspaper also give a sense of other things going on in the world at the time politically, economically and socially.

Google, Twitter, Facebook and forums have yielded important and useful information generally, as well as introducing me to contacts who knew Clapham in the 1970s, and a few who actually recalled the Rose and Crown pub and my father. If the internet had not been invented, there are many things that I would never have discovered.

I tried to avoid paying for information on ancestry and genealogy websites with the odd exception here and there. My coffers were not unlimited and I had to spend money.

There are any number of books available on tracing family history, but if you're on a limited budget why not use your local library. You might also want to look at parish records, cemetery registers, military archives and education registers. If you are lucky enough (I wasn't) to find family diaries, letters and photographs, they would be wonderful sources of information and insights. I suppose if there is one thing I have learned in all of this, apart from the fact that I should have got off my backside years ago to do this research, is to keep things that might not seem important at the time but could be of significance in the future. I am old-school in that regard and favour shoe boxes to safeguard memories. Modern technology allows us all to photograph and digitally record and archive our lives and the lives of others.

In addition to all the archive digging and search engine activities, there was nothing else for it but a train trip to follow in my father's footsteps. Of course, it's difficult to compare Clapham now with what it would have been like back in the 1970s, but most of the buildings are the same and I got a good feel for the area.

Researching takes time but I believe it's worth it. I know much more about my father and my wider family than ever and I feel good about that.

CHRONOLOGY

1925	Birth of Margaret Mary 'Rita' Millar (my mother).
1925	Birth of John Cushnan (my father).
1947	Marriage of Rita and John (my parents).
1949	Birth of my brother Paul.
1950	Birth of my brother Sean.
1951	Birth of my sister Mary.
1952	The Cushnan family moved across Belfast from the New Lodge Road to Andersonstown.
1952	Birth of my sister Geraldine.
1954	I was born.
1955	Birth of my sister Sheila.
1958	Birth of my brother Kevin.
1960	My father left our Belfast home and never came back.
1970	I left school and got a job with the Belfast Corporation Electricity Department.
1971	I joined Stewarts Supermarkets, Belfast, as a trainee manager.
1973	I joined British Home Stores (BHS), Belfast.
1973–1982	My father (as John Kelly from Derry), lived in Clapham, London.
1974	My brother Paul was killed in a road accident in Scotland.

1976	I moved from Belfast to various branches of BHS in England.
1980	I got married.
1982	My father died, aged 57, in the National Hospital, Camden, of an intracranial tumour.
1984	My son David was born.
1984	I joined Alfred Dunhill Limited, London.
1986	My son Steven was born.
1987	I joined the Bolton Abbey Estate, North Yorkshire.
1989	I joined Makro Self-Service Wholesalers, Liverpool, then Sheffield and Nottingham.
1992	I graduated with a BA (Hons) from the Open University.
1995	I joined Asda/Wal-Mart in Derby, then Leicester, Mansfield and Leeds.
2005	I worked as a freelance trainer and writer.
2007	I joined Frank Thomas Limited, Northampton.
2008	I retired from full-time employment.
2011	My mother died, aged 86, at her home in Bingnian Drive, Belfast from senile dementia and debility of old age.
2018	My brother Sean died aged 68.

ACKNOWLEDGEMENTS

I am very grateful to the following people and organisations for support, encouragement and help in various degrees:

Alyson Wilson, The Clapham Society
Belfast Newspaper Library
Damian Smyth, Arts Council of Northern Ireland
David Walden, Lambeth Cemetery
Derrick Johnson, The Clapham Society
Fr. Michael McGreevy, St Mary's Church, Clapham
Gail Walker, *Belfast Telegraph*
General Register Office of Northern Ireland (GRONI)
Gerry Kelly, BBC Radio Ulster
Helen Tovey, *Family Tree* magazine
J. P. Devlin, Aasmah Mir & Reverend Richard Coles, Saturday Live, BBC Radio 4
John Toal, BBC Radio Ulster
Kevin John Dean, Southsea Lifestyle
Linda O'Reilly, The Anglo Celt
Michael Bradley, BBC Radio Ulster Arts Show
'Peter'
Peter Jefferson Smith, The Clapham Society
'Sue'
The Arts Council of Northern Ireland
The National Lottery

and, of course, members of my family:
Mary Moorehead, Geraldine Higgins and Sheila Butler, my sisters, Kevin Cushnan, my brother, Sheila Faloon, my mother's sister and various others who threw in little titbits here and there.

Thank you to my editor, Averill Buchanan -
https://www.averillbuchanan.com

Selected sources that informed, enlightened and assisted the writing:

Death of a Naturalist by Seamus Heaney (Faber and Faber, 1966)

An Unconsidered People: The Irish in London by Catherine Dunne (New Island, 2003)

The Kings of the Kilburn High Road by Jimmy Murphy (Oberon, 2001)

Aftermath: On Marriage and Separation by Rachel Cusk (Faber and Faber, 2012)

And When Did You Last See Your Father? By Blake Morrison (Granta, 1993)

Not My Father's Son by Alan Cumming (Canongate, 2015)

TransAtlantic by Colum McCann (Bloomsbury, 2014)

Kelly: A Memoir by Gerry Kelly with Don Anderson (Gill & MacMillan, 2008)

Life on the Limit by Jenson Button (Blink Publishing, 2017)

Cyclone: My Story by Barry McGuigan (Virgin, 2012)

Clapham in the Twentieth Century by The Clapham Society (2002)